Speak Out!

Speak Out!

Talking About Love, Sex & Eternity

Dawn Menken, Ph.D.

New Falcon Publications
Tempe, Arizona, U.S.A.

International Standard Book Number: 1-56184-152-8
Library of Congress Catalog Card Number: 00-111487

First Edition 2001

Cover Art by Andrea Courvoisier
Cover by Amanda Fisher

The paper used in this publication meets the minimum requirements of the American National Standard for Permanence of Paper for Printed Library Materials Z39.48-1984

Address all inquiries to:
NEW FALCON PUBLICATIONS
1739 East Broadway Road #1-277
Tempe, AZ 85282 U.S.A.
(or)
320 East Charleston Blvd. • #204-286
Las Vegas, NV 89104 U.S.A.

website: http://www.newfalcon.com
email: info@newfalcon.com

Acknowledgements

This collection was truly inspired by something greater than myself. To this spirit that moves me, I am eternally grateful to be alive and to follow the mystery of life that leads me.

This book could not have been written without my association and friendship with Arny Mindell. I have absorbed his teachings with a hunger that can only be matched with my overwhelming gratitude for his being, his love for me, and his awesome spirit that has inspired so many people throughout the world.

I want to thank the following friends who have contributed to this book with their feedback and ongoing encouragement: Jan Dworkin, Amy Mindell, Kate Jobe, Randee Levine Cathey, and Julie Diamond. I want to acknowledge the late Markus Marty for the inspiration and financial help he gave me to begin this work. I am greatly indebted to my editor, Leslie Heizer. Her encouragement, skill, and kindness definitely brought this work to the light of day.

I also appreciate all the learning I have received from the worldwork community, which consists of individuals from numerous countries and diverse cultures working on the challenging social issues of our times and risking emotionally as a large learning community. I have learned so much from the worldwork gatherings that are portrayed throughout this work.

My beloved partner, Renata Ackermann, has been as solid as the mountains she comes from in her love and belief in me. It is this atmosphere that enabled me to write. At the same time she has been a constant challenge to my work; her love of learning and dialogue made for many an interesting interaction. I must also acknowledge Eli, feline extraordinaire, who always made his rounds by my computer at the right moment, offering purrs of affirmation and captivating me with his joyous antics and uncanny wisdom.

Contents

Forward

Dear reader, Dr. Dawn Menken's *Speak Out! Talking about Love, Sex and Eternity* inspires you to think about your deepest beliefs and the way in which you relate to this world. Dawn's personal stories give you a living experience of the spirit of Taoism, and its reflections in process work (or Process Oriented Psychology, as it is called in Europe and Asia). She shows how worldwork, an inner and outer method of working with groups, may be lived and incorporated into everyday life. For her, democracy is not just a concept, but a lifestyle, a moment to moment awareness project. Dr. Menken's book shows how this awareness can work in a day to day, practical manner.

By speaking about her personal life, she shares the most intimate experiences and relationship processes. She speaks about partnerships, her relationship to god, and her connection to culture. Sexuality and sexual identity are gently explored as altered states of consciousness. Gender issues, sexism and the many faces of marginalization, including racism, anti-Semitism, appearance and homophobia/heterosexism, are discussed.

Her special touch is given to personal experiences of process work and its appearance in large community worldwork seminars. Her insights and descriptions address unresolved diversity issues from history, present difficulties, and possible solutions to problems of our global future. Her ideas are not only thought-provoking, but poetic. Hope you enjoy this work as I have.

Arny Mindell
Yachats, Oregon 2001

Preface

In November 1994 I was in Slovakia at the annual worldwork seminar sponsored by the Global Process Institute.[1] Eastern Europe was changing rapidly after Russia had begun to loosen its hold and the Berlin wall had come down. Slovakia and The Czech Republic had recently become two nations and people were finding their voices after having lived for decades under the yoke of domination. Two hundred and fifty people from all over the world gathered together for two weeks to focus on the issues of our time, learn about conflict and group work, and create community from the awesome and unpredictable experiences that occur when so many people from various nations and cultures congregate.

In this atmosphere, in a worldwide learning community, in the midst of intense interaction around issues of race, gender, economics, sexual orientation, anti-Semitism, and fascism, I dreamed that I gave birth. Seconds out of my womb, the infant looked directly at me and spoke, "Write a book on love, sex, and eternity." Never has a dream been so clear and directive to my conscious mind. This work is a product of that calling.

I have often wondered why the baby immediately spoke, When I remember the awesome experiences I had in Slovakia, I will never forget the first days when eighty Slovaks and Czechs sat silently while western voices dominated the seminar. I was thrilled when revolution broke through this unconscious power and fresh voices flooded the floor. Indeed, the interactions in our seminar mirrored those of the world at large. The topic shifted its focus to the precarious political situation in Slovakia where an old-time communist puppet had just been elected. Most people were terribly distressed and feared that Slovakia would return to communist control. I was inspired by the courage of the Slovaks in speaking up, going against decades, and in some cases lifetimes, of tight social control that had infiltrated the deepest core of emotional and individual expression.

Days later the sexual minority community penetrated a wall of silence and oppression expressing the pain and anger that comes from enduring marginalization for loving someone of the same gender. I found myself speaking out in the midst of great adversity, standing for the eternal nature of love that knows no boundaries.

The worldwork seminars are incredible forums for speak outs, a time when various voices are heard uncensored. It is no wonder that I birthed a baby who also wanted to speak. This work is my speak out. The opinions and views are my own and do not represent any other marginalized person or group. Individuals who speak from the position of a marginalized group are often taken by the mainstream to reflect all of the ideals and viewpoints of that group. Groups on the margin reflect great individual diversity, just as difference of opinion is reflected in the mainstream.

The reader will find a voice that stands for love in all of its multitudinous displays. This work reflects on relationships, sexuality and intimacy, and their interface with culture, psychology, and spirituality. The eternal drive for freedom and liberation is echoed throughout. The essays also comment on a variety of social issues. In addition, this work is moved by the eternal yearnings of the spirit to learn and love, to feel connected to the heartbeat of the universe. Some pieces are autobiographical, some academic, and some in a poetic style. Through stories and personal experiences, this work reflects and comments on the spirit of our social, political and cultural times.

This collection comes to press as we have entered the new millennium. This momentous time is infused with the power of our greatest hopes and fears. It is a time for new visions to emerge and fresh voices to be heard. It is a time for each of us to speak out and also to listen to the many voices out there. I hope to encourage and inspire each of us to speak out, to tell our stories and share our experiences as inspiration and learning for others.

End Notes

[1] GPI is a non-profit international organization that focuses on education and research in regard to applying process work to social and world issues in an attempt to work with conflict and create world community. Process work (also known as process-oriented psychology) is a unique school of psychology devel-

oped by Dr. Arnold Mindell, with wide applications and roots in Jungian Psychology, Taoism and modern physics. Worldwork seminars focus on diversity work and community building with large multicultural groups and have occurred in different countries since 1990.

Introduction

In 1979 I went to Zurich, Switzerland where I studied with Arny Mindell, founder of process-oriented psychology (process work). I lived there for over ten years and participated in the development of this innovative and comprehensive psychological system that works with a wide range of human experience, including body symptoms, extreme states of consciousness, comatose and near-death states, and relationships.

Since 1990, process work has seen the development of worldwork, which focuses on processing social issues and large multicultural group interactions. Worldwork grew out of process work theory and is a revolutionary method that uses psychological tools and awareness to address diversity in group settings. In a typical worldwork seminar, an international group of about 300 people gathers to create community out of conflict, diversity and the unpredictable experiences that groups constellate. The atmosphere at these events is often hot and emotional. Marginalized groups conflict openly with the mainstream, and momentary resolution arises out of emotional changes in the group itself. Individuals and groups that are typically not given a public voice are encouraged to speak out.[1]

Worldwork is a unique blend of psychology, social action, and awareness principles that culminates in greater community understanding. I have learned so much at these worldwork events that much of this writing has been inspired by the interactions and reflections that occur during and after these profound encounters. During these events one witnesses the power and community spirit of individuals and groups that have been excluded from society. Listening to these voices, I have been touched to the core by the courage, depth of emotion and celebration of the human spirit under oppressive circumstances. I have been left shaking and in tears; I have been furious and I have been overwhelmed by love. I have been deeply moved, beyond what I know in myself and into the hearts of others. This movement generates something like a spiritual center for groups and creates the seeds of community life. Community grows out of the sharing of new experience, emerges by staying close to the edge of what is known. This is the pulse of group life, the mystery that moves hearts when both the individual and the group experience themselves anew.

In community life, a fundamental root of conflict can be traced to the unconscious powers of the dominant segments of any given group and the voices that are disavowed, cast out, and deemed insignificant. Worldwork embraces this key dynamic by creating a powerful forum for interaction. *Speak Out!* is a tribute to the many voices that have been marginalized, voices inside of myself as well as others. At the heart of process work and the practice of worldwork lies the basic principle of deep democracy, which addresses this perennial conflict of marginalization by emphasizing the value of all viewpoints and the necessity for them each to find expression. This is essential not only for group, social, or political life, but inner life as well; often inside of us there is tyranny in the way we disavow or exclude aspects of our experience and cement identities that inhibit us from expressing our expansive natures.[2]

Often those of us who have been marginalized lead the group or the world with the depth and personal power that develops through living in a society that doesn't embrace us. During the worldwork seminars it is often the African Americans, Native Americans, Aboriginals, women, gays, lesbians and bisexuals, Jews, Latinos, Eastern Europeans, those from less industrialized countries, those who have known hunger and poverty and collective abuse, those who have lived under dictatorship, communism and fascism and various others who have come forward with their fury and pain, courage and compassion, breaking through our mainstream slumber.

These individuals fascinate us; they throw us off balance, knocking us out of our comfort zone. We are captivated by their experiences and awed by their power. From a mainstream perspective, we also feel outraged to be awakened. We can't listen; we don't want to. We want to hold onto our known worlds, the powers we know, the place where the world is safe and secure, the ground rules that we have created and expect everyone to live by. This interaction lies at the heart of personal, community and world change.

This work is infused with the living spirit of process work and its worldwork applications. The thinking and feeling are inspired by its viewpoint, which respects and follows the nature of life's unfolding. The personal essay format allows the reader to experience how the basic philosophical principles of process work theory and worldwork are translated into everyday living. Process work is an attempt at a "living Taoism," a psychological system and spiritual philosophy that inspires us to follow the Tao or to discover the mystery and unknown in everyday life. This work is not a theoretical book about process work;[3] however, the essays do reflect core spiritual beliefs and worldwork principles that are embedded in personal experience.

The first piece introduces the reader to some of the basic dynamics between marginalized and mainstream groups and gives the reader a peek into the worldwork seminar in Slovakia that was referred to in the preface. Other writings make some reference to worldwork gatherings, and much of the work addresses themes of marginalization, the quest for freedom and learning and growing together as a world community. Besides my own experiences and learning that permeates this book, as a therapist and teacher of process work, I use case examples to make the situations I am addressing more real. Most essentially, many of the writings in this work explore the deeper spirit behind worldwork: love, relationship and community, and the eternal drive for learning and divine connection.

Process work and worldwork have been part of a greater evolution in psychology that brings together psychological thought with spiritual beliefs and social justice issues. Psychology can no longer afford to separate itself from the urgency of social justice issues nor can it be devoid of spirit or meaning. *Speak Out!* is a tribute to this deep well of learning.

End Notes

[1] For an in-depth study of worldwork see the following books by Arnold Mindell: *Sitting in the Fire* (Portland, OR: Lao Tse Press, 1995) and *The Leader as Martial Artist* (San Francisco: Harper Collins, 1992). For an overview of a typical worldwork seminar see Leslie Heizer, "The Worldwork Seminars: A Personal Learning Overview," *Journal of Process Oriented Psychology* Vol. 5 No. 1(1993) 5-12.

[2] Arnold Mindell coined the term "deep democracy" and discusses central democratic ideals and principles in political life, community interaction and also in our inner lives. See *Sitting in the Fire* (Portland, OR: Lao Tse Press, 1995) and *The Leader as Martial Artist* (San Francisco, Harper Collins, 1992).

[3] For books about process work, please refer to the books by the following authors: Arnold Mindell, Amy Mindell, and Joseph Goodbread. Many of these books are cited throughout the text.

Reflections of a Social Activist[1]

Steve Kopek thought he was a lesbian. At least that's how it appeared. Every time we saw him stroll across campus with a few of his avant-garde lesbian friends, drooling on Georgia, we knew that he not only wanted her, but wanted to join the movement that she was a part of.

It was 1976 and I was attending a radical liberal arts college in the Midwest. The sexual revolution had taken hold; AIDS was yet to come, and gay life was becoming more visible. African American Studies and Women's Studies departments sprouted up in universities, and support groups flourished as various marginalized subgroups formed their own communities.

I will always remember the first time I stepped into the Gay Center. The entire campus was abuzz with the news of the Saturday night dance at the Gay Center. I wondered why this would generate so much excitement; after all, every Saturday and Wednesday the school held the best dances I had ever been to. "Gays give the best parties," I was told.

I didn't know where the Gay Center was and at the time felt quite intimidated to go near it. I wondered what it would have meant about me, about my identity, if I had begun making regular visits. As I walked through the balmy night I was surprised to find all sorts of people strolling at the edge of campus, approaching a rundown wooden house that seemed to visibly vibrate from the distance.

The place was packed, the music was loud, and the atmosphere was warm, colorful and sexy. No one at the door checked to see if I belonged or not, no one investigated what my sexual identity might be. In fact, no one seemed to notice or care who was identified as gay, lesbian, bisexual or heterosexual. The atmosphere embraced everyone. On this turf gay men easily danced with each other and their straight brothers, and all sorts of women moved together, blurring the borders of sexual identity.

I spotted Kim. Her elf-like glance enchanted me and I felt my heart beat faster. She was the first lesbian I had personal contact with, and she took it as her personal task to orient me to various altered states and experiences. I hadn't slept with a woman yet, and she enjoyed my interest and flirted with my fear. With her easy and confident way she swept me onto the dance floor. The wooden boards moved beneath my feet and the house shook in time with the music and gyrating bodies. "We are family," we all sang out with the Pointer Sisters, and we really felt it.

Steve Kopek really irritated me. A white, male, heterosexual college student, filled with unconscious privilege, pretending that he was a lesbian feminist? What was he trying to do? Spouting feminist theory, lusting after a woman who so obviously had no interest in him and disowning his social identity. It took me many years to understand Steve. In the meantime I connected with an old friend who confessed to me that he too had often fantasized about being a lesbian. He felt lesbians had more intimate relationships and felt drawn to the community feeling amongst lesbian women.

That community feeling made parties at the Gay Center exciting and intimate events that drew large numbers of people from outside the gay community. This special kind of community functioned outside of mainstream morality, luring anyone who wanted more contact with parts of themselves that had been collectively constrained. The desire for freedom compelled many to join this community that had already risked existence outside collective acceptance and had felt the fear and ecstasy of having to stand alone. Those who identified as straight could go to such parties with minimal risk to their identity and could simultaneously experience the thrill of sexual freedom, flirting and dancing with their own edges.

What attracted me to step foot into this "forbidden" gyrating building? Deeper than the sexy atmosphere and beneath the mysterious aura, I had never experienced a situation that welcomed such diversity. I was captivated, compelled and terrified to explore my own inner diversity and expand my identity, and that dancing building opened its doors and whisked me in.

I noticed then that marginalized groups often become the hub for community life; there is a special spark that becomes at once appealing and also threatening to the mainstream. Over the past few decades in the United States numerous marginalized groups have become more visible, creating strong grassroots communities that have influenced social and cultural life as well as public policy. Marginalized groups have a lot of power in the communities they create and many of us in the mainstream are drawn to this power.

Worldwork and the Magnetism of Marginalized Groups

When I went to my first worldwork seminar I was reminded of that night at the gay center. I recognized an atmosphere where people stepped into the unknown, flirted with the boundaries of their personal and social identities, and interacted with diverse cultures and individuals in a more or less supportive environment. Worldwork creates an unusual forum where community gathers, marginalized groups have the rare chance to express themselves, and the mainstream listens.

In such a forum it becomes clear to the dominant group that those who have been discounted have incredible powers that have been sorely neglected. Those in the mainstream are often drawn by these powers, by the unbending drive for freedom that vibrates in the heart of a life shaped by marginalization and oppression. Those in the mainstream are captivated by the hard-won ability to speak out and stand alone, by the depth of experience that comes from having to survive and use all of one's inner resources when the outer ones are denied or unacknowledged.

Spiritual Rank and Marginalized Groups

No matter how we react as the mainstream and what ensues when conflict and difference are processed publicly, it is increasingly clear that there can be a tremendous power in belonging to a marginalized group. Living in a world that excludes you could be seen as a powerful invitation to develop in truly awesome ways. Don Juan Matus, the Yaqui Indian shaman chronicled in the books of his apprentice, Carlos Castaneda, explains this paradox in the lives of his people.

> Indians are the losers of our time. Their downfall began with the Spaniards and now under the reign of their descendants the Indians have lost everything.... One can easily surmise that for the poor average Indian the reign of the white man has been sheer hell. And yet the irony is that for another kind of Indian it has been sheer bliss.... The sorcerer. For the sorcerer the Conquest was the challenge of a

> lifetime. They were the only ones who were not destroyed by it but adapted to it and used it to their ultimate advantage.[2]

Through the worldwork seminars, where social issues of power and oppression are addressed, Arny Mindell noticed that the power of the mainstream was largely unconscious.[3] Those of us who are part of the mainstream in a given moment are not necessarily aware of our powers and privileges, nor do we necessarily feel them. I say in a given moment because being part of the mainstream or of a marginalized group is a relative concept. When issues of racism emerge, everyone who is white is part of the mainstream, even if they are also women, Jewish, gay, or poor. At the moment when the gay, lesbian and bisexual community speaks out, everyone who lives a heterosexual lifestyle is part of the mainstream. The unconscious nature of mainstream power becomes shockingly clear when a marginalized group expresses itself and the mainstream suddenly looks weak. The power of social rank crumbles as the mainstream seems unable to match the emotional and psychological strength of the marginalized group or individual.

Mindell explains these group and social dynamics in terms of a ranking system that describes the various kinds of powers which create the sense of status and value in our society and relationships.[4] The most obvious rank is connected to social status. If one is male, white, and heterosexual one has a lot of social rank. This status is a result of social convention and is therefore not earned by the individual. More difficult to perceive and understand is the more subtle rank based on spiritual, psychological or emotional power. This kind of rank is developed by the individual, earned by hard work, life experience and personal growth. Don Juan says that these personal powers are untouchable and cannot be stolen or taken from the oppressed.[5]

Mainstream Envy

What really drew Steve Kopek to the lesbian community? He was jealous. It wasn't that he really wanted to be a lesbian—he wanted the inner powers and spiritual rank represented by an oppressed group. Those who possess this spiritual or psychological rank are often the natural leaders of a group. They are teachers, not only about diversity and prejudice, but about the human spirit. They model courage, show a wide range of emotional depth, speak truths, and at times demonstrate unbelievable compassion and generosity towards mainstream ignorance.

As much as the mainstream envies the spiritual rank and community feeling generated by marginalized groups, the mainstream must be careful about how it deals with its jealousy. Spiritual or psychological rank is the only rank that has been available to those disavowed by society. Value and power are earned by the blood, sweat and tears of transforming incredibly oppressive circumstances. Unchecked mainstream envy can unconsciously be seen as an attempt to take everything from the marginalized individual or group.[6] It is inadvertently another act of genocide, attempting to steal the very soul of the individual or group.

Although this spiritual or psychological rank can never really be taken, how we in the mainstream deal with our envy is nevertheless essential. By developing our own spiritual rank, we honor oppressed individuals by taking them as teachers. If we do not take this as a chance for our own growth but compete with their power, if we use our social rank to oppress their spiritual power, or if we attempt to benefit by association, we become part of the oppressive system. For example, in the political sphere in the United States, the far right has introduced legislation in many states that discriminates against gays and lesbians. The organizations responsible for these measures fear the power they see in the gay movement. They claim there is a gay political agenda they need to act against. In a way this is true. The gay, lesbian and bisexual population has a desire, or an agenda, to have the same legal protections as heterosexuals and to enjoy the same social liberties.

Considering the present outer legal and social situation, mainstream values still rule. This could make one wonder what the far right fears. It is true that in the last 25 years the gay movement has come into its own as a small political power, which is slowly influencing public opinion. However, more than this, the root of their power lies in the inner experiences and beliefs of a group of people fighting for the right to love whomever they choose. The spiritual rank that many of these "warriors" display, and their unmoving certainty in standing for love and freedom, creates a power that is impossible to legislate against. I believe it is this core power that truly frightens the mainstream. Such power is seen as a threat and is enviable to those who have relied solely on the power of social rank.

Internalized Oppression and Spiritual Rank

The mainstream identifies those of us who are marginalized as inferior, and too often we believe them. However, like don Juan, some of us take this fate as a strange gift, knowing that we are faced with the incredible challenge of developing beyond both our internalized oppression and an outer society that is hateful and oppressive. Paradoxically, these threatening and oppressive circumstances often create ripe ground for personal development. It is when we are most unbalanced and least secure, when our identities are under threat, that we must reflect and develop. At these times we search for meaning in the incomprehensible. We grow beyond the parts of ourselves that only suffer, and are forced to expand beyond the identity that the mainstream has laid out for us. This is no easy feat. Those of us who belong to groups that have been oppressed know all too well the agonizing internalized racism, homophobia, sexism, and classism that we are forced to deal with.

A Chance for Mainstream Development

When the mainstream feels threatened by a marginalized group, it gets a small taste of the attack that marginalized groups constantly suffer. Frequently the mainstream responds in defense and anger. However, the mainstream has also stumbled upon an opportunity for development, for it is exactly these conditions that have enriched and empowered those who have been put down. It is a challenge to awaken from our mainstream slumber and foster the kind of inner rank so often idolized or feared in oppressed groups. Jung would say this is the call to individuation. He claimed that the process of individuation began when one separated oneself from the collective, from accepted societal norms and beliefs and embarked upon a process of self-discovery outside of collective opinion.[7] Attacks from marginalized groups are often aimed at our unconscious acceptance and perpetuation of mainstream values. Such criticisms help us discover our own inner powers by pressing us to reflect on the mainstream trance that we have unwittingly supported.

The Personal is Political: Discovering World Tasks

Not only surviving but flourishing under attack, using painful and oppressive circumstances for inner development, is one of the central elements that creates spiritual or psychological rank. When our existence is threatened, we are faced with existential dilemmas about the meaning of our lives, and whether we really want to live or die. During these times many of us discover how our personal lives are inextricably connected to world tasks or basic universal longings. We become more connected to some greater purpose. This awareness gives us enormous spiritual rank.

When an African American stands up in a group and speaks about her daily struggles with racism, she talks not only about herself, but a universal longing for freedom. Her individual struggles are not only personal. Her personal life takes on great meaning as she stands for essential human matters. This struggle gives meaning to the expression, "the personal is political." Here, psychology and politics come together.

Individuals who derive inner powers from terrible oppression stand for essentials like freedom and love. This is what makes these people so attractive to the mainstream, what draws Steve Kopek to his lesbian friends. It is an ecstatic experience to stand for core issues and to feel that our lives are driven by something greater than our individual selves. This is one of the greatest benefits of the worldwork seminars. Not only does the large group have the chance to learn about various issues and differences and interact around them, but individuals are given a chance to develop themselves in the context of a large diverse group that mirrors the outer world.

Worldwork and Personal Growth

We often think of our personal growth as something that happens privately, through inner focus, meditation and reflection, or therapy. However, one whole area of personal work happens only in the context of a large group or community atmosphere. Worldwork seminars have been particularly valuable in acknowledging that psychological growth takes place publicly in the turmoil and interaction around social issues.

Worldwork seminars, town meetings and other community gatherings offer individuals a chance to speak out. The common person has little opportunity to be heard in the world. Public speakers are usually political leaders, famous people or leading social activists. Rarely do mainstream and non-mainstream groups engage in any kind of dialogue except political posturing. Marginalized groups often experience the mainstream as a faceless mass that determines social policy and insidiously permeates every aspect of daily life. A worldwork forum provides a chance to meet face to face with the collective personality that haunts daily existence.

Too often therapy reduces social pain to unresolved personal issues. In the confines of the therapist's office one cannot interact with real external forces. Public interactions, such as those that can happen in a worldwork gathering, are essential to bring out parts of ourselves that otherwise don't emerge. Watching a dear African American friend of mine stand up strongly and awaken a white male to his unconscious racism moved me deeply. I also remember a man from Sweden bursting into tears when he realized how his lack of awareness around racism had inadvertently caused so much pain. I remember a woman from Germany coming forward at a time when no one else would, healing the hearts of many as she suffered and took emotional responsibility for the acts of her family and country during the Second World War. I will never forget the spirited group from Slovakia standing publicly against fascism. It was moving to watch the courage it took the group to overcome its deep-seated fears about speaking up after so many years of oppression.

Our growth happens publicly in such interactions, and we grow internally as we discover our ability to hold various viewpoints at once. Some of us develop a certain feeling of detachment after having gone through so much emotional upheaval. With this feeling we find ourselves able to support various viewpoints. As Mindell says, we become elders for the group, looking out not only for our own position but for the entire group as one body.[8]

Worldwork 1994: Slovakia

During the two weeks of worldwork in Slovakia, we focused on many issues, including racism, colonialism, dictatorship, sexism, and conflicts between Eastern and Western Europe. Every worldwork seminar has thrilled and challenged me, pushing me into new areas of personal experience. The seminar in Slovakia gave me an experience of my own learning and growth around rank and detachment. Following are my reflections on one of the last mornings of that seminar.

The atmosphere was tense as a lesbian woman came forward and asked the group to focus on homophobia. We were in Eastern Europe where there is no strong political gay movement; homosexuality is rarely mentioned and according to the mainstream, doesn't exist. At this particular seminar, many people from Eastern Europe and Russia had never met a gay person, and many people in the group felt other issues were more important. Even in places where there is a gay movement, homophobia and gay rights are easy issues to push aside. This inflames the gay community, which often feels invisible and neglected. We finally reached consensus when a man from Slovakia implored the group to focus on an issue he knew might appear strange, but is one through which he has learned much.

A group of gays, lesbians, bisexuals and allies gathered on one side of the circle. I noticed the surprise of many group members as individuals who don't fit gay stereotypes took personal stands. The silence erupted into passionate voices expressing emotions about years of oppression. The large group was challenged to look at its own homophobia, at how it can maintain an oppressive atmosphere through holding unconscious beliefs about homosexuality. The gay group felt the unexpressed thoughts and feelings of the mainstream and wanted them voiced to provide a chance for interaction. As the two sides conflicted, the polarity in the group that had hung heavy in the atmosphere was manifest, and the two positions continued in a heated debate.

Gradually the more overt and painful beliefs about homosexuality were expressed. "Homosexuality is not normal." "It's a phase you are going through." "It's a psychological problem." "God is against homosexuality, it's a sin." These statements were met with a variety of emotional responses. A Baptist minister came forward preaching the anti-gay sentiment his church upholds. "God created Adam and Eve, not Adam and Steve." The larger group laughed and a lesbian woman furiously admonished the group for laughing at something so painful. Another minister spoke about the difficulties he had in his so-called liberal church, where there is an atmosphere of tolerance, but not true inclusion.

I wondered where I belonged in this process that day. I was watching the scene before me; I was part of the group that holds the pot, offering focus and attention so the process can continue. This was not the first group process I had experienced on this topic. In the past, I have been the social activist. I have screamed my heart out in anger, cried in pain and been ready for battle. I have been confrontational, begged for understanding and stood for love in the midst of incredible hostility. I have welcomed the chance to express emotion and engage in direct public confrontation. These awesome experiences have left me trembling with vitality and have helped me contact parts of myself that I didn't know existed.

I noticed I was not as emotionally moved as I usually am. I wanted to do something to help the group process along. Polarities had formed,[9] and I felt a need to interact differently with the homophobic position. Something had shifted inside me; I had burned so much with anger in the past that I noticed a more detached feeling. I felt I had something to bring to this group process, but I was not yet sure what it might be. I was waiting to be moved, for the spirit to call me forward.

A group stood together voicing homophobic thoughts that are rarely spoken. One man revealed, "I have always had this fantasy that if I could sleep with a lesbian I could change her." The other side of the room exploded, exasperated and furious. Suddenly I was propelled into action. I desperately needed to respond, although I still felt strangely detached, almost friendly. I felt something powerful inside, and I was shaking as I took the microphone. The room was suddenly quiet as I faced off with this man.

I looked at the man, whom I knew, and waved from across the room. "Hi," I said, smiling, slowing down the pace, not reacting in the expected confrontational way. "Hi," he said, taken slightly aback. I took a long look at him.

"You are a sexy man," I said. He blushed, looking at me sheepishly. "Thank you," he replied, obviously embarrassed.

I went on, "Just as I find you sexy, I also find women incredibly sexy. Love and sexuality are not cognitive processes. We don't think about who turns us on, about the gender of the person who draws us. We can't will ourselves to be attracted to someone. These experiences are beyond what we consciously choose. Love and sexuality are magical and mysterious, taking us into some of the deepest parts of who we are. It is an electric experience to be so powerfully drawn to someone that we must follow those feelings wherever they take us. These are some of the most intimate and beautiful experiences we can have in life, divine impulses that are meant to be nurtured and worshipped."

The room was silent, listening intently. The man across from me relaxed, nodding as if he understood something. We exchanged a warm look. Then suddenly a man next to him stepped forward and added, "But what about a penis? You need a penis for fulfillment."

I studied this man and took the microphone again. "It is a great and ancient belief that the penis is the fulfillment of all things to everyone in every way." The room exploded with laughter as this was translated into Slovakian. I noticed that I was enjoying myself, feeling very detached and free to say the unspeakable. I continued and addressed him personally.

"I think your penis is gorgeous." The group howled and the man smiled. "And so am I when I get all excited and turned on. I want to live that feeling wherever it takes me. That kind of energy has no boundaries, no morality. I feel it is the deepest and most mysterious thing in life, something that should be cherished and followed. I think it is a sin to go against it."

I sat down, shaking and excited. The group was moved, and the atmosphere had changed. The polarities had relaxed and the large group decided to split into small groups where individuals could talk more personally and work intimately on issues around homosexuality.

Not only was the group moved, but I was. Something had happened to me, came through me. I didn't know who I was anymore; I was enjoying myself in a struggle that I usually find excruciating. It was freeing to not only be furious, although I have also enjoyed my fury and value its expression. I am sure that I could only do my part because other sisters and brothers were carrying that emotional reaction. It was teamwork, and I was free to experience something new, something outside my normal repertoire.

Even though in this scenario I was part of an oppressed group, I felt I had incredible powers. I felt my spiritual or psychological rank and I enjoyed using it. I welcomed the opportunity to stand for love and its holy nature and to talk publicly and personally about sexuality. In that moment, I felt untouchable. No one, no matter how antagonistic or cruel, could hurt me.

Conclusion

Spiritual or psychological rank is available to all of us regardless of color, class, gender, religion, age, health or sexual orientation. Paradoxically, this inner feeling of value might be more available to those of us who have been socially oppressed, because access to other external status has been limited. Mainstream jealousy reveals the need for all of us to develop our deepest nature.

The ability to grow inwardly, experiencing value through personal development, is a gift, and may even be a calling. In fact, most great religious and spiritual leaders spend years cultivating themselves, seeing their inner development as the highest achievement in being closest to the divine. I believe it is a spiritual undertaking to use whatever life hands us to further our own inner work. In order to do this we must truly see the meaning in all things, see that all experience holds the seeds for inner growth.

With this view, we can transform anything that comes our way. This view of life does not exclude social activism. I do not advocate for a world where injustice is passively accepted, but feel that working on oppression also means reaping the inner benefits from having to deal with such pain. Individuals who have traveled this path are the perennial teachers of all time, for both the oppressed and the mainstream.

End Notes

[1] First published as "Somewhere Over the Rainbow: The Quest for Spiritual Rank," *The Journal of Process Oriented Psychology* Vol. 7, Number 1 (1995) pp. 27–33.)
[2] Carlos Casteneda, *Tales of Power* (New York: Simon and Schuster, 1974) 138–9.
[3] Arnold Mindell, *Sitting in the Fire* (Portland, OR: Lao Tse Press, 1995).
[4] Arnold Mindell, *Sitting* Chapter 3. I am indebted to Arny Mindell for all of the learning around group process dynamics and rank issues between the mainstream and marginalized groups. Many of the ideas presented here are culled directly from my learning from him and the group processes that I have seen him facilitate or study.
[5] Castaneda, *Tales.*
[6] Max Schupbach articulated this insight during a multicultural group process at the Process Work Center of Portland in the winter of 1995, in Portland, Oregon.
[7] C.G. Jung, *The Collected Works of C.G. Jung, The Archetypes and the Collective Unconscious,* Vol. 9, Part I, Bollingen Series XX, (Princeton: Princeton University Press, 1959).
[8] Arnold Mindell, *Sitting* Chapter 13; Arnold Mindell, *Leader as Martial Artist* (San Francisco: Harper Collins, 1992) 156–60.
[9] Polarities exist in every group and in group process work the facilitator attempts to bring these polarities into the foreground so they can interact directly. See Mindell, *Leader as Martial Artist* and *Sitting in the Fire* for more information about polarities and group roles.

The Best for You

"Whatever makes you happy," says your father, looking a little less elated than he did moments before when you told him about your gay relationship. If whatever makes you happy makes him happy, he should be dancing and jumping for joy about the great love and excitement you feel! You find yourself wanting to run away; your mind spins trying to understand the mixture of his caring words and glum mood. Bodies twitch, eyes scan the ground; the discomfort is palpable. "That's good Dad, I *am* happy," you manage to voice, not sure why you must stress it since he says he is happy for you. "I'm glad," he says, unconvincingly and barely audibly. Your eyes find the door and you can't wait to be released from this grip of grief and doom.

"I only want the best for you," laments your mother, unaware that she is mourning what would have been best for her. "It will be so hard for you." How often have we heard such statements from caring family and friends and how often have we uttered these same words to our loved ones? These statements are commonly heard in the coming out stories of the sexual minority community. However, similar phrases are uttered whenever any one of us forges our own path and steps outside mainstream guidelines.

History is full of painful and heroic stories about all sorts of individuals who had to leave families, cultures, nations and loved ones to follow what was closest to their hearts. Buddha's parents thought he was crazy to give up the life of luxury into which he was born. Jesus had to defy his culture and religion, venturing out to follow his calling. At one time or another most of us have had to go against cultural or family beliefs, against what might have been thought best for us.

What is the best? Does the best mean the least painful, the easiest, the safest? Is the best the path with least conflict or obstacle, or risk? Is the best what the majority agrees to? Is the best what brings the most financial profit? According to many of our families and the cultures we live in, a life with minimal risk that upholds the status quo is considered optimal. However, which is really less painful—developing and embracing all of ourselves or adapting to societal expectations and cutting off a huge part of our experience?

Moderation and Extremity

All over the world, cultures tend to avoid extremes and support a middle ground. Although cultures differ, each culture has a norm that inhibits behavior seen as outside cultural constructs.[1] We want things easy and settled, and most of us want to adapt and be like everyone else. Those who differ from the prevailing norms are locked up, ostracized or not accepted into society. Too often the best is bland; we value moderation and don't easily welcome that which appears odd, extreme or volatile. We have spoken and unspoken rules that keep us all relatively compliant.

The desire for moderation, for the safety and comfort of a predictable lifestyle, is important and seems to be a natural human drive. For those of us who live in cultures and countries where there is little safety, this drive seems especially essential. Nevertheless, no matter what our outer circumstances, stepping outside our cultural security is a huge break in consensus reality. Despite this, most of us, at one time or another, are compelled to do so.

Although we try, many of us are unable to keep within cultural borders. Dreams, creative inspirations, relationships, inner experiences, spirituality, and desires for freedom and justice propel us over the edge of our safe and familiar reality. An often neglected drive is our extremity, the desire not only for comfortable survival but also for intensity, transformation and full expression of all possible experiences. This drive remains neglected insofar as we are not aware of it and attempt to maintain inner and outer culture as we know it. We develop parts of ourselves that our culture supports and marginalize other aspects that are seen as less desirable. We create culture in the same way by elevating some citizens and cultural behaviors as the norm and marginalizing others. We then hold everyone to these one-dimensional standards, inadvertently enforcing them by the limited representation of individuals and possibilities in government, education, media and economic status. Culture is maintained by everyone striving to attain these standards in order to succeed in a one-dimensional world. Making it in the mainstream is valued as the best. No matter what our background, those of us who are successful in making it assume that culturally valued success is also the best for others.

However, culture itself evolves, led in part by eruptions from those who have been marginalized. Marginalized groups and disavowed parts of ourselves cannot be indefinitely stifled. Our wholeness is irrepressible and the more we inhibit its expression, the more violent the outbreak.[2]

Conflict Work[3]

Our peace agreements do not hold because agreement based only on maintaining the status quo is not inclusive. Viewpoints considered more extreme by culture will eventually create dangerous perimeter groups, not because the message is necessarily dangerous, but because it has been shut out and must use any method it can to be heard.[4] Conflict can never be resolved by marginalizing any part of the conflicting system, whether that be world conflict, group conflict, relationship conflict or internal conflict. Each party must be fully invited into the arena and be able to completely express itself, or it will reappear and disrupt any solution.

Keeping the peace has too often meant that one nation, individual, culture, religion, race, gender, morality, or inner part of ourselves dominates and others submit. Real peace can never be built on submission, where one party might temporarily surrender its power, viewpoint, character or personality. Disavowed individuals, groups, opinions and behaviors make themselves known; they appear in revolutions and riots, in our dreams and body symptoms; they are locked up in our psychiatric clinics and live on the streets of our cities. They are expressed in the violence of our marginalized youth and in the altered states evident in our craving for drugs, alcohol, cigarettes, coffee and painkillers.

Historically, we must know this. Every generation has witnessed the fury and retaliation from a nation, group or community that has been dominated by a stronger power. We know that we cannot really shut out or exterminate a part we do not agree with because it will return in some form. If our method is to overpower those who are different by force, legal means, emotional or verbal powers, or by our insidious beliefs and institutionalized powers, we do not create a sustainable society, but propagate a breeding ground for revenge.

But we behave as if we do not know this, because when the vengeful party returns we do not see what brought him to this violent point and we do not open up to his marginalized message. Instead we condemn his behavior, protect our position, and attempt to eradicate him. The cycle continues.

Opening up to difference is an ancient and urgent challenge. Our drive for security seems to foster a viewpoint that familiarity, predictability, conformity, and homogeneity make a safer world. Difference threatens that perceived comfort, but it needn't. It is not comfortable or settling to be constantly warding off difference. With so much diversity in inner and outer life, security can never be achieved in isolation. We must learn to interact and get along with difference. It is almost trite to say because many of us have been told or taught this. However, our parents and teachers and the world around us rarely model it. We wall ourselves off with borders and militias, while we legislate certain ideologies and criminalize others. We stay in familiar groups, maintaining ignorance and fear of those who seem strange. We disavow parts of ourselves that we find unusual or unappealing, and insist on our opinions and perceptions as if they were the only ones.

But how could we be otherwise? Mainstream cultures instill in us the idea that there is one reality, one viewpoint, one right answer. Few of us have been taught that many truths can exist simultaneously. Diversity threatens our view of reality, and we begin to wonder who we are. In our desperation and panic we are all in danger of becoming fundamentalists. If we lack options to deal with difference, we must insist adamantly on our reality.

Learning

We cannot secure ourselves against difference. Those who are made impotent by majority domination will become as fundamentally insistent as the domineering majority viewpoint. This is obviously dangerous. The viable option is learning to exist in the chaos and uncertainty of a society with many viewpoints and to conflict in a way where each party is enriched rather than defeated.

I was never taught that I could learn from conflict, that conflict might be a wonderful opportunity to discover more about myself and the world around me. Like many, my experience of conflict was of winning or losing. I had to fight fiercely for fear of being dominated, and hence the only option was to dominate the other. Since then I have learned that the crucial attitude in getting along with difference is the desire to learn. Conflict and difference are opportunities for great discovery.

But something in us doesn't want to learn. It is afraid. Difference stretches us, takes us outside of what we know. It upsets the world as we know it and from this perspective we only experience the threat and discomfort of our reality crumbling. If we believe in one set reality, it is devastating to appreciate and learn from difference. However, if we know we are evolving fluid beings, difference becomes an awesome opportunity for transformation. We still might be afraid as we stand at the threshold of a new experience, but we are also inspired to explore ourselves.

When we encounter differences in the world around us we are challenged in our inner development. To allow another viewpoint means we must open up to that part of ourselves. Let's take the example of a gang member. For those of us who do not identify as gang members, when we are confronted with gang activity in our neighborhoods, we condemn it and mobilize our communities to deal with the "gang problem." Those of us in suburban neighborhoods separate ourselves even further by seeing the "gang problem" as an inner city issue, entirely outside our domain. In either case, we do not realize that the gangs are parts of us too.

Can we not only understand the viewpoint and social alienation that the gang experience has emerged from, but can we also discover that psychologically we too are somehow gang members? This is why we dream of these individuals, and why we have such strong reactions when we hear about them. We are not separate from the experiences of wanting to belong and feel powerful. We are not unlike the gang members who feel that they need to defend their turf. Instead of doing a drive-by shooting, some of us will kill our competition by less direct and more sophisticated means, which will have the same devastating effect. When we have been rejected numerous times we too get desperate and will sometimes engage in risky or ethically questionable activities, whether that be in our business practices, in how we handle finances or lie about our work experiences. In these times, we are not unlike the millions of marginalized and disenfranchised youth who have repeatedly been denied access to job and educational opportunities because of the color of their skin or ethnic heritage, and who are then forced to make it in the drug world. When we as the mainstream know that we are them, we might deal with this issue very differently. We will see that we cannot just condemn, standing outside of the issue thinking that we know best. We will see that we are not separate and changes will emerge from appreciating and understanding this shared psychology.

Colonization

State and federal governments in the U.S. think they know how to best deal with gangs and drugs. They convince the public that we need more jails and stiffer drug sentences. "We need to crack down on drugs and violence," says every politician hungry for votes. The underlying issues of racism, classism, lack of educational opportunity, and mainstream cultural domination are neglected in the politician's surveillance of the problem. White upper class men who are removed from this reality make most of these decisions and neglect crucial social factors. They honestly think they know best, that their lifestyle is the only one worth emulating, and that their knowledge can save the rest of us.

This is colonization. It is no different than European and American countries invading others, often under the guise of helping, and insisting on their cultures, behavioral norms, technology, language, religion, aesthetics and way of perceiving the world. Colonization is more than the invasion of land or resources. The colonization of thinking occurs when insidious beliefs infiltrate every aspect of culture and behavior, thus maintaining a sense of superiority that has no knowledge and experience of, or relationship to, other ideas and people.

Colonization is the action of racism. It is the unconscious superior belief that we are the best and others will even invite our dominance. Colonization happens every time we insist on our viewpoint as the way for everyone without consulting and appreciating the other person. It happens every time we remain on the outside and make decisions for others.

Internalized Colonization

Most dangerous is the often subtle colonization of behavior or of our inner or cultural psychology. When a black mother tells her extraverted and joyous children to be quiet so white folks will value them, this is a rape of the spirit. When Jewish people assimilate for fear of standing out, we have created a tyranny of behavior. When gay people inhibit their natural expression of love and affection so as not to be offensive, they live with chains around their hearts. When Native Americans feel they must abandon their roots and prove their intelligence, we destroy the ancient wisdom of indigenous peoples. When women restrain their emotional expression so they are valued in a rational society, we have lost the heart of human nature. When any group of people feels that they have to alter their behavior for fear that it will reflect badly on their race or group, we have colonized a sacred aspect of being human.

Inner Work

We have not only created a social ranking system[5] based on ethnicity, race, religion and gender, but a hierarchy of behavior. Rational, linear, subdued, balanced, moderate, kind, and articulate are some of the qualities that are at the top of this hierarchy in the United States. Individuals from marginalized groups are then identified with behavior that is outside of these parameters, such as emotional, sexual, aggressive, loud, ecstatic or irrational. They are identified with this disavowed behavior not because they don't possess the standardized behavioral qualities, but because the mainstream only sees those qualities that stand out from their model. In fact, the mainstream needs marginalized groups to carry these disavowed behaviors because it is unwilling to claim them. This is obviously hurtful to those from marginalized groups who suffer the pain and exclusion of objectification and are not seen as individual beings with a whole range of qualities.

Behavior that the mainstream deems inferior is projected onto marginalized groups. The mainstream colonizes itself, partitioning off behavior that then remains inaccessible except in the form of stereotypes and prejudices. Since the mainstream removes itself from certain behaviors, stereotypes become a way of unconscious disidentification from particular groups of people. However, we in the mainstream, no matter how educated and knowledgeable we are, cannot easily free ourselves from these stereotypes unless we reclaim them.

This is the painful horror; we in the mainstream use those whom we have rejected in order to rediscover parts of ourselves. This is why many of us in the mainstream also feel attracted to and sometimes envious of individuals from marginalized groups. They are doing things and behaving in ways that we too would enjoy, but culture has cut off our natural access to these abilities in ourselves. Our dreams at night are filled with a diversity of people in order to connect us with the projections that we have on them.

From my work with people, I remember the white woman who dreamt of being chased by a black man and needed to get in contact with her own power and intensity. The man who made an unconscious cut about Jews succeeding in business needed some of the business savvy that he projected onto Jews in order to save his failing venture. The older female board member of a psychological school who looked down on lesbians needed to connect with her own tenderness. The white American man who dreamt of a Japanese woman needed the modesty that he saw in her posture.

The majority culture must retrieve what it has split off and disowned. Bland and compliant is not the best; it limits everyone's growth and objectifies many of us. It is not enough to vicariously experience ourselves through the projections we have onto others. Each time we watch the parade of stereotypes that runs across our television and movie screens, we are called to discover those behaviors in ourselves. The media profits because we in the majority culture sit back and pay for it. But who really pays for it? Those of us outside the majority culture pay more than our share. We pay daily by the constant objectification that the media maintains, which limits our freedom by chaining us to those images, and thus restricts us from opportunities in the job market and prevents us from being valued for all of who we are.

As a therapist, I constantly work with the immense drives and passions of the human spirit and the borders of cultural domination. At this crossroads the mixture of excitement and freedom, terror and condemnation, are obvious. "It's too weird," a client says, grinning from ear to ear. "I can't be that wild!" he exclaims, hardly able to contain his excitement. "I can't stand out like that," she says puffing her chest out, looking for me to encourage her. This is what we are all like at the edge of our own comfort zone, stepping out into the unknown, beyond cultural approval. We fear that culture will reject us, our relationships will change, we'll lose our jobs or someone will lock us up. But somewhere we are thrilled and looking for comradeship, knowing that expanding our worlds and letting our spirits soar would truly be best for us all.

End Notes

[1] See Arnold Mindell, *City Shadows: Psychological Interventions in Psychiatry* (London and NY: Routledge, 1988) for more on the relationship between culture and extreme states.

[2] This is a basic premise of process-oriented psychology. Arnold Mindell demonstrates how disavowed aspects of ourselves manifest themselves in dreams, body symptoms, relationship conflicts, altered and extreme states of consciousness and in group dynamics.

[3] For a thorough introduction of conflict work and an elaboration of the following ideas, see Arnold Mindell's, *Sitting in the Fire* and *The Leader as Martial Artist.*

[4] See Arnold Mindell's *Sitting in the Fire,* chapter 6, for a discussion on terrorism.

[5] See Arnold Mindell's *Sitting in the Fire,* chapter 3, for a complete discussion on rank, power and privilege.

Looking for God

I am looking for God. I look up and around me and I see hundreds of people dressed in their finest, surveying who else is present and catching up on all the latest news. No sign of God yet. Maybe when we all sit down, I will see or hear or even feel the presence of the holy one. It is September, the time of the high holy days, "the most important holidays of the Jewish religion," my mother tells me.

The lace around my arms itches and my tights cling too tightly to my legs and hang down in the crotch. I am trying to hold my legs together so no one sees my panties. We are sitting on hard wooden chairs and I am looking up at the cavernous ceiling. I have never seen a ceiling this high except at the circus last year. My eyes scan each corner and crevice wondering when God will pop out.

I forget about keeping my legs together and sit on my heels trying to see where the booming voice is coming from. Over the sea of heads I quickly spot a man in a black robe, and then my mother tells me to sit properly. I listen carefully; it sounds like he is calling out to God. I hope God hears him. The man in the black robe begins to speak in words and sounds that I don't understand. "Is this a special secret language that he has with God?" I wonder. I am anticipating God's arrival. Surely, God will hear us now. My eyes roam the room; I want to see the moment He appears.

The voice up front drones on. My vigilance is suddenly interrupted by the strange singing of another voice, again in this secret language with tones that make me sway. The long notes vibrate inside me. I have a funny feeling in my chest and stomach. It's all tingly and empty like it wants a hot chocolate to fill it up. "Is God swimming inside of me?" I wonder.

I look up and around; there is still no sign of God. Adult eyes are staring at me; they smile and point at my cute new dress. I see other kids squirming in their seats, cranky and pulling on parents. Older kids seem to be eyeing each other, trying not to giggle, engaged in some secret language of their own. It is easy to catch someone's eye; most people let their eyes wander the room freely except for some of the older men who have their heads buried in books and mumble along with the voices coming from the front. Occasionally, everyone joyously sings together and is permitted to stand up and stretch their limbs.

The feeling in my stomach and chest is now gone and I am bored. My clothes are bothering me and I want to go home. God didn't show up. No one seemed to mind. That tingly empty feeling inside haunts me, pulls me to it like the smell of fresh baked chocolate chip cookies, except it sounds like breathing with a rhythm that pulls on my skin.

It was Wednesday afternoon. That meant me, two other Jews and a Protestant spent the last hours of school alone with the teacher while the rest of the class walked the block to St. Anthony's for religious instruction. I didn't mind these afternoons; I usually did an art project, got a head-start on my homework, or the teacher gave me some job.

At three o'clock I rushed out into the fresh air. The kids from church were walking up the hill spilling over with laughter and excitement. I wanted to join them and wondered what had everyone going. Carol cried out, "Could you believe Michelle confessed that she gave twenty-one guys a blow job! I couldn't believe it. I would have given anything to see the Father's face."

Michelle was a year older than I was, but seemed even older than that. Boys teased her a lot and I don't think I ever had a conversation with her. Standing at least five heads away from Carol, I chimed in with my disbelief and horror. I don't think anyone heard me or even acknowledged my presence. I got on the school bus and went home.

At 5:30 my father gave his daily call to say he was leaving work and should be home in an hour. He asked me how my day was. "It was okay, except Michelle Gaglione confessed that she gave twenty-one guys a blow job!" I blurted out. There was a deafening silence on the other end of the phone. "Dawn, do you understand the meaning of what you just said?" My face began to get hot and I felt caught in my ignorance. "Sure I do," I weakly asserted. "We'll talk about this when I get home tonight," he said. That night my father never said a word about it and neither did I.

Confession was a big mystery to me. I couldn't believe you would tell a holy man your most private thoughts. I wanted to do it too and I finally got my chance. Confession became a part of our games. My friends and I often played school and frequently it was Wednesday. We had to go to religious instruction and I got to know the nature of nuns and priests; I learned how to say the Our Fathers and Hail Marys, but most of all I felt what it was like to be so intimate and vulnerable in the face of God.

December intrigued me. The whole town was decorated and lit up. One block in particular was strung with so many lights and displayed so many Santas and nativity scenes that my brother and I stretched our necks whenever we drove by. The lights were beautiful and glamorous, but I was fascinated with the nativity scenes. I watched as Sicilian grandmas carefully placed the three kings, Mary and Joseph and of course the baby Jesus. Men and women suddenly appeared so reverent before these plastic figures, kneeling down and crossing themselves. I could never imagine my own parents worshipping a baby.

It wasn't until my late twenties that I understood what intrigued me about Catholicism. Walking out of the ancient, stone archway of a Swiss church one Christmas Eve after midnight, images from my youth flooded my mind. How could these people worship a baby, I wondered. A baby with so much power. A baby who was a God! I let it sink in—people worshipped a baby. Big strong men and women who seemed so self-sufficient with all the answers prostrated themselves before a baby.

I could see this Catholic God in the figurines, on the crosses and in the artwork. But most of all I saw this God in the way people were emotionally affected. He made adults cry, brought the most macho of men to their knees, and made women's eyes mist over in their love for Him.

Catholicism showed me the sacred nature of human emotion. Baby Jesus, who moves hearts and minds and brings the mighty to their knees, taught me humility. Someone up there knew what she was doing when she made Jesus a human being; how else would we know our humanity is divine?

As a teenager, I dreaded September. Summer vacation was over and I knew those high holy days were just around the corner. I could see no sense in going to worship. Services felt hypocritical to me, like a big fashion show. No one in my family believed in God, and for them, as for many reformed and conservative Jews, the religion of Judaism held little passion. In the height of furious arguments with my parents, I challenged my father. "Why do you go to temple if you don't believe in God?!" "I go to be counted," he said defiantly. I saw pain and determination in his face, the history of a persecuted people.

At the time I couldn't see the spiritual significance of his assertion. It took me many years to discover that at the heart of Judaism lies the quest for freedom and a burning passion for social activism. No wonder so many Jews I knew were social activists. No wonder my favorite holiday was Passover. Besides the great food and gathering of family and friends, Passover celebrates the liberation of the Jewish people from the chains of slavery.

Reading Michael Lerner's ideas about Jewish identity helped me appreciate this aspect of Judaism and offered an explanation for why so many Jews seemed disconnected from the Jewish religion but deeply connected to its cultural roots and sociopolitical history. According to Lerner's understanding of the Torah, Judaism is based on transformation. The world is not a set entity, created and complete, but a divine being in the process of developing. Human beings are partners with God, are meant to assist world change, and have a religious obligation to strive for universal freedom. Therefore, Lerner reminds us, the most common injunction in the Torah is, "When you come into your land, do not oppress the stranger. Remember that you were strangers in the land of Egypt."[1] These simple sentences affirm the sacred unity of all people and the universal desire for freedom.

The God of the Old Testament implores us to know that we are the other, insists on our divine connection to each other. If we neglect one another, we neglect a part of ourselves. This frequently overlooked viewpoint is a central key to resolving conflict and appreciating differences in all relationships and all peoples, thus underscoring the divine calling to social action. God treasures freedom and emphasizes the religious obligation that each of us has to ensure it. Thus, the legacy of social activism in the Jewish faith is central to its spirituality.

I was five the first time it happened. I was lying in bed and couldn't sleep. The traffic was loud but the thoughts inside my head were deafening. What happens after we die? If we die, why are we here? Why would

God create people only to kill them? What does God do with us after he creates us? Does he play with us like I play with my dolls? What happens to love when we die? Why would God create love and then take it from us? Why does God keep creating people if they only die? Is there a time when all the people die and no one else is created?

Three days earlier John F. Kennedy had been assassinated. I walked home from kindergarten in tears. I vowed to myself that when I died I would wake up JFK, his family, and my family and reunite us all.

Even though the Old Testament promises an afterlife, a paradise with the coming of the Messiah, the Jews I knew asserted that death was the end. In fact, they insisted that Jews don't believe in any kind of afterlife. The spirit died with the body and any other viewpoint was seen as irrational. Modern-day Judaism seemed very rational and scientific, its earlier roots long forgotten.

Catholics and Protestants spoke confidently about heavenly reunions, even though grief about a death seemed to consume everyone. People in my world seemed to be very connected to this life on earth; death was feared and experienced as a tragedy. Death took from us. It didn't enrich, but deprived. This cultural climate generated the disbelief and question in my five-year-old brain of a God whose ultimate act of creation would end with such devastating finality. That sense of shock and disbelief has stayed with me throughout my life, pushing me to grapple with the purpose of existence and my task on earth.

A culture that emphasizes one reality so adamantly cannot conceive of other realms—in life or in death. Therefore, it wasn't until I began to have experiences that were outside of consensus reality that death seemed less ominous to me. Other worlds did exist—they were always there if we could perceive the doors that stood before us. Our dreams and body experiences and all of the strange and unpredictable events that occur every day are paths to these altered states.[2] Many European Americans in the 1950s bathed in the certainty and homogeneity of one reality, while many in the following generations experienced this same reality as a prison. The tremendous appeal of Eastern philosophy and religion, native spirituality, shamanism, body therapies, drug use, yoga and meditation that proliferated in Western culture were lures into other worlds. A world so unpredictable couldn't be so one-dimensional; many longed to experience more of the mystery.

In 1994, on a warm summer evening, I stood with thirty others around the bed of Markus, a friend who had just died of AIDS. From the outside looking in you would never think that we were standing around a dead body. Death wasn't supposed to be like this—or was it? We sang, rejoiced and laughed. We told stories and celebrated a man whom we had all loved dearly. We shared the experiences we had had with him, particularly his last year of life. We had learned so much from and around him. We would miss him, but we were also happy for him. Death wasn't just evil. In fact, the process of dying had transformed him, given him incredible experiences that were gifts to us as well. Dying opened up other realities. Markus died before he died in that he had begun to strip off his attachments to consensus reality and free his spirit. In this world, love, nature and God were his guides. Every setback in his physical life became a great learning.

Months before his death, Markus came home from the doctor very depressed. According to the doctor, his recent seizure indicated that he was going downhill fast; dementia had snuck up on him and he was going to lose his cognitive faculties and become totally dependent. An articulate and highly intellectual man, dementia had been his biggest fear, and now the medical authorities were confirming it. I went to visit him that evening and sat with him on his front porch. He looked at the sky and told me everything was all right. The sky held his gaze and tears filled his eyes. He whispered to me, "It is so beautiful. I can't explain it, but I feel totally at peace. This is bliss. I have never felt so well in my life." I had nothing to say, but felt healed in his presence. We sat together hand in hand looking into the heavens. His dementia never incapacitated his spirit. Up until the end of his life we were able to communicate with him and learn from him.[3]

One day I was sitting with Markus in a public square. A middle-aged woman sat across from us. He asked if her left leg was okay. I couldn't see anything particular about her left leg or about her at all for that matter. She was startled and visibly moved by his contact. She told him she had hepatitis and a lot of pain in her leg. The boundaries of relationship had lifted; Markus spoke with anyone who moved him, disarming them and creating meaningful relationship. Relationship was not wasted on superfluous speech, but each interaction seemed to reach into the soul connecting with the deeper spirit between people. In altered states such as his, new worlds of relationship open up, which allow us to dream into other people and give us "psychic" abilities.

With less attachment to life as we have known it, dying seems to bring us into other realms and altered states of consciousness, which enrich the dying person as well as those around her.[4] If we look at death only as a mechanistic breakdown of a failing body, we deny the richness of these experiences. Mainstream culture doesn't mean to devalue other-worldly experiences; it is just that we marginalize them daily in everyday life, so we also don't perceive them at death. From this viewpoint, death is a tragedy; an end to the one reality that we have known and upheld. When we experience the gifts of altered states and other realities as Markus did, death cannot be seen only as a loss.

In India, death seems to be an integral part of daily life, visible and ordinary and at the same time sacred and mysterious. In the holy city of Varanasi, I watched as dead bodies wrapped in bright orange cloth were carried on bamboo stretchers through the narrow streets to the cremation ghats on the Ganges. People hardly noticed, just as people hardly noticed the numerous extreme and colorful individuals who make up the complex and rich tapestry of India. India seems to be much more open to and familiar with the diverse states of consciousness that life and death offer us. Being immersed in a culture where life and death mingle as close friends, I had the strange thought: In India there might be no mid-life crisis. The concept of mid-life crisis seems to emerge from a Judeo-Christian orientation and a Western industrialized culture which values youth and production, dismisses the gifts of age, and neglects the great diversity of various states of consciousness and experience that can appear in all ages. Lack of contact with altered states in life fosters the fear of death, which from my outsider's viewpoint seemed to be a non-issue in India. Our view of death contributes to how we experience the process of aging.

On the banks of the Ganges I watched the bodies burn. Holy men and family members carefully engaged in a purification ritual that included first dipping each body into the water and then setting it on a pile of wood. The body took three hours to burn and the remains were then cast into the Ganges. This sacred river was home for all spirits in transition. I was awed by the public display of death. Around one funeral pyre I watched a group of men and boys exuberantly dancing and singing. The celebratory atmosphere reminded me of our time with Markus. Eight distinct fires burned and I saw no one who appeared to be grieving.

The profound detachment of the Indian people made a deep impression on me. Hindu philosophy asserts that this life is not all there is, and that spirits return and can connect with others. This viewpoint seemed to give the Indian people a great tolerance for the difficulties and challenges of living and dying.

The self-determination and urgency so prevalent in my culture seemed absent. Instead, even in the midst of so many people, there was a sense of ease or relaxation. The contrast made me giggle one afternoon. I was sitting on an airplane waiting to depart from Varanasi when the pilot announced that there was an air traffic controller's strike. All around me Indian people sat patiently without protest. I imagined the scenario in any airport in the United States and watched this inner drama unfold. Huffy individuals pushed forward, insisting on information and lamenting lost time. Voices were raised in panic and I heard the desperation and frustration that emerge when the will is thwarted by the unpredictability of circumstance. Looking inward, I recognized that the part of me who makes my plans does not like to be thwarted and likes to reign supreme. Simultaneously I noticed I was delighted by the one who giggled upon hearing the pilot's announcement and relaxed into the next adventure that life was providing.

Over the years I have been moved and altered by my personal and academic encounters with Eastern thought and religion. This detached world view offers a relativistic viewpoint that embraces the paradoxes inherent in the dualistic certainty of Judeo-Christian thought. Such detachment and relativity come about when we believe our lives and universe are not final and that we are part of a larger evolutionary process. If we are constantly evolving and our spirits continually reincarnating, how can we become so attached to only one physical manifestation of our spirit? If we know that human experience is limitless, how can we become hooked to only one part of ourselves?

With this in mind it is easy to grasp the great diversity of Gods and Goddesses in the Hindu pantheon. I was tickled by a story related by the theologian, Diana Eck. She met a Hindu elder, called Uncle, who asked her about Christian beliefs.

> "Is it true," Uncle asked as if verifying an outlandish rumor, "that Christians believe Jesus was the *only* avatara?" [Loosely translated, an avatara is the divine embodiment of God that descends to earth for a purpose.] ..."Yes, most Christians do," I responded. "Christians say he was unique, the only one." "But how is it possible," he asked, "to

believe that God showed himself only once, to one people, in one part of the world, and so long ago?" The implications were clear on Uncle's face: What kind of stingy God would that be? What kind of small-minded, self-centered people would believe in such a God? To him it was clear that the full, embodied disclosure of God to men and women was not only multiple in time and place, but potentially infinite.[5]

When I returned from India, my aging Grandmother had become quite ill and we all feared this might be the end. Perhaps the effects of India inspired the dream I had after a week at home. I was in my Grandmother's house. She took me in her arms and told me that I was very special to her and that she had always been the protector of my spirit. She then began to sing an old Yiddish song that I did not know. I understood the word *schaenala*, my beautiful one or child. She told me that she would always be with me and I should not worry about her dying. I looked at her and her skin changed radically; her wrinkles disappeared and her skin became smooth and started to glow. Then she was gone.

I awoke quite startled from that dream, feeling that it was her goodbye to me. I never felt closer to her. I felt her inside of me whether she lived or died. From this perspective Grandma is an eternal spirit who will always be with me. India reinforced the great interconnection of spirit and the relativity of living and dying. There is too much mystery in this universe to think about living and dying so conclusively.

Perhaps my childhood wishes are valid. Maybe I can awaken those I love—when I am dead and when I am alive. And just maybe, love does continue.

My earliest recollection of Taoism is the image of Chinese sages with their gaze fixed on some distant horizon beyond the immediate happenings of everyday life. Stories of crazy wisdom and profound paradox twisted my brain and made me giggle, while the *Tao Te Ching*,[6] which sounded like the poetry of the universe, revealed the beauty of nature and the deepest mysteries of creation. But reading the *Tao Te Ching* is completely different than experiencing life's seemingly unpredictable and nonsensical teachings.

It isn't so simple to detach from everyday troubles. One of my earliest lessons in detachment came in my early twenties, during a battle with one of my dearest friends. She had cut off our friendship and I was suffering and hurt. One night I dreamt that she was right. I awoke totally distraught. How could someone who had been so mean and rejecting be right? My inner belief system of right and wrong was shaken. There were no clear absolutes; my emotional certainty was being contradicted by my dreams. I felt like I was reading a Taoist proverb or a Zen koan. What did it mean that she was right?

My whole world began to shift. I realized that life was a world of lessons, that "rightness" had more to do with the way of nature and learning than it did with any one set of morals or principles. Being right was not connected to a single emotional viewpoint, but in the learning that one acquired from the interaction of various viewpoints. The richness of living had more to do with how we met life's challenges and less with our luck in avoiding misfortune.

Awake in the night, I struggled with this seemingly ancient dilemma. My dream-life was suggesting a certain humility. My ears began to buzz and I heard a voice. "Humility has nothing to do with being right or wrong, with winners and losers, being less than or better, it has to do with being humble to what is happening between people, to the ways of nature." This unusual voice in the night gave me an old time lesson in following the Tao. Something relaxed inside me. My suffering was relativized and I felt able to approach my friend in a new way.

In poetic verse, the *Tao Te Ching* captures this humble attitude:

50 Bowed down then preserved;
Bent then straight;
Hollow then full;
Worn then new;
A little then benefited;
A lot then perplexed.[7]

The paradox and wisdom of Taoism captivated me, but it was difficult to apply it to my everyday reality until I began to study process-oriented psychology (process work), which opened me up to the reality of a "living Taoism." It attempts to follow the flow of experience as it manifests itself in various perceptual channels like movement, vision, audition and feeling, and also includes the information that presents itself in our relationships and outer environment. Process work follows the Tao that cannot be named by exploring individual experience without labels, interpretations or goals.[8] Individual experience speaks for itself on its own terms. By working with subtle signals that lead to direct experience of our dreaming, nature presents various viewpoints, thus balancing our one-sidedness and embracing the paradox of mystery and change inherent in the teachings of the Tao.

Recently, I sat with an estranged friend who had betrayed me. She repeatedly apologized and I heard a child's voice inside of me say: "But how could you do that to me?" I let the Tao of the moment take me, repeating my question with an innocent voice and my face full of tears. How difficult it is to really follow the flow of nature and emotion, to let a child emerge in the presence of someone who has been so hurtful, and yet the voice in my ear was a piece of nature wanting to come forward. I watched her struggle for words, beside herself with the pain she had caused, at a loss to remedy the damage that had been done. She stroked her legs and shyly said that she wished she could comfort me.

I was holding my head in my hands and noticed my face get hot as I became aware of a signal that was pushing itself into my awareness. I noticed my head leaning towards her. "What was it doing?" I wondered. I tried to open up to the experience happening in my leaning head and discovered a part of myself that would let her comfort me, that longed for her to hold my head. I struggled with the new information. "How could I place my head in her hands?" It was easier to just be furious, justified in my hurt and anger, and not let her close to me.

Process work calls this a "double signal," an aspect of myself that I have marginalized and do not identify with, that expresses itself outside of my intentions.[9] Therefore, my dreams at night reveal this aspect of me, and this dreaming leaks through in waking life, expressing itself through body signals.[10] Double signals have the potential to melt conflict or dissolve stalemates by introducing new possibilities into our interactions. From the perspective of our identity, double signals bring up the absurd and unpredictable, that which cannot be discovered by cognitive methods. From the perspective of the Tao, there is no judgment, it is simply the way.

The judgments and hesitations of my identity momentarily faded as I let myself be taken by the Tao or dreaming process between us. I inched my chair closer to her and leaned my head into her trembling and receiving hands. The emotion and improbability of the moment transformed us both. A part of myself stood outside of the interaction, awed that I could drop so much personal history. I felt elated and unattached, unburdened by any form of myself, free to do and be anything. There was no consequence to any action, no permanence, just a moment's expression of the Tao and the naked truth between us.

Double signals lead the way to the seemingly impossible; they regulate our one-dimensional viewpoints and point to directions not previously considered. Double signals remind us that we are all potential Taoists. Why? Because they inform us that we are not absolute and disclose the "rightness" of following nature. By following and unfolding the signals of our inner nature with great attention we become fluid beings, unpredictable and open. To become like water is a Taoist metaphor for living life.

> 186 In the world there is nothing more submissive and weak than water. Yet for attacking that which is hard and strong nothing can surpass it. This is because there is nothing that can take its place.[11]

Taoism still teaches me about the wisdom and mystery of the universe and to follow the flow of nature's endless and meaningful expressions. It inspires me to be fluid, to identify myself as more and less than what I think I am, and to know that there are many sides to everything, that nothing is absolute because everything is relative. Nature teaches me to change because change is the only constant. Taoism shows me the divine in what is discarded by teaching that the journey or the way itself is God. To be open as a newborn and yielding as water is a way to meet life and death. This attitude has helped me to know that even in the midst of turmoil and fear there is learning and wisdom. That the Tao, that God, the great spirit, the dreaming world or whatever name or concept you choose, is in me, in you, in the trees, animals and plants, in our interactions and conflicts and what we disregard and marginalize. Indeed, God is everywhere.

End Notes

[1] Michael Lerner and Cornel West, *Jews and Blacks* (New York: Grosset/Putnam, 1995) 9.
[2] See Arnold Mindell: *Working with the Dreaming Body* (Boston and London: Routledge and Kegan Paul, 1985); *City Shadows: Psychological Interventions in Psychiatry* (London and NY: Routledge, 1988); *Coma: Key to Awakening* (Boston: Shambhala, 1989); and *The Shaman's Body* (San Francisco: Harper, 1993).
[3] For more on communicating with people in comas and near death states see Arnold Mindell, *Coma: Key to Awakening* and Amy Mindell, *Coma: A Healing Journey* (Portland: Lao Tse Press, 1999).
[4] See Arnold Mindell, *Coma: Key to Awakening* and Amy Mindell, *Coma: A Healing Journey*.

[5] Diana Eck, *Encountering God: A Spiritual Journey from Bozeman to Banaras* (Boston: Beacon Press, 1993) 82.
[6] Lao Tzu, *Tao Te Ching,* trans. D.C. Lau (New York: Penguin, 1963).
[7] Lao Tzu, *Tao Te Ching,* trans. D.C. Lau (New York: Penguin, 1963) 79.
[8] See Arnold Mindell, *River's Way* (Boston and London: Routledge and Kegan Paul, 1985) for a deeper understanding of Taoism and process work.
[9] See Arnold Mindell, *Working with the Dreaming Body* (Boston and London: Routledge and Kegan Paul, 1985) and Joseph Goodbread, *The Dreambody Toolkit* (London: Routledge and Kegan Paul, 1987).
[10] Mindell, Arnold, *Dreambody: The Body's Role in Revealing the Self* (Boston: Sigo Press, 1982).
[11] *Tao Te Ching* 40.

Ties that Bind Us: The Spirit of Relationships

The Face of Marriage

There was a time in my childhood when the worst thing I could imagine was my parents getting a divorce. A folk song about a father telling his children the tragic news used to haunt me; it stuck in my mind and could make me cry. Years later I sometimes wished my parents would divorce. Their unresolved conflicts hung in the air like the heavy smell of fried liver. I watched them tiptoe around the difficult spots in their relationship and I never saw them resolve an issue.

As I climbed in years, so did the number of divorces in the United States. The old people lamented that things weren't how they used to be, while the morality police claimed that the sacred institution of family was breaking down. They blamed the women's movement, the sexual revolution, the hippies, punks, and gangsters, the drug culture, interracial marriage, immigration, welfare, teen pregnancy, and homosexuality. Such comments were made as if the only family that existed was white and middle class, consisting of a man, woman, and a couple of children.

Segregation, racism, native genocide, unconscious white supremacy, sexism, heterosexism, and the dominance of puritanical European values hypnotized the majority culture into thinking that family life should mirror the 1960s television prototypes of "Leave it to Beaver" and "Father Knows Best." Although lifestyles have expanded considerably in the last four decades, there is little real representation of a wide range of relationship and family life in the media. Furthermore, what is presented often fuels various stereotypes and myths. In particular, African American families have had to fight the myth perpetuated by the media that the black family in the United States is disintegrating. Dr. Andrew Billingsley, prominent author and renowned researcher of the African American family, discredits this myth and praises the strength, community, and incredible endurance of a people faced with the everyday obstacles of racism and the enduring residue of slavery.[1] In the 1980s single parenting faced strong public criticism, and a myth developed that equated black family life with single, teenage, unwed mothers. Unconscious racism has perpetuated this myth and Billingsley reveals the facts. "Most single parents are adults, not teenagers. Most are white, not black. ...teen parenting among white girls in America—leaving aside black girls altogether—is higher than in any of the other industrialized Western countries."[2]

When we look outside white European culture, we find family styles that are not reflected in the statistics. Billingsley asks, what is the African American family? "[I]t is an *intimate association* of persons of African descent who are *related to one another* by a variety of means, including blood, marriage, formal adoption, informal adoption or by appropriation..."[3] Appropriation, a bond highly valued in African American culture, refers to ties without blood or marriage. "People can become part of a family unit or, indeed, form a family unit simply by deciding to live and act toward each other as family."[4] The concept of appropriation in which relationships are created by intent and not blood is not found in family statistics, yet these bonds are highly valued by many of us. The tribal family style of Native American culture has also been overlooked.

Furthermore, when studying marriage and divorce, it is important to remember the history of these institutions. The institution of marriage is based on the ownership and acquisition of women. Slaves were forbidden to marry.[5] Gay and lesbian relationships and families have never been acknowledged and currently fight for the right to marry and adopt children, in addition to keeping their own biological children. When we talk about relationships, the statistics of divorce, and the nuances of family relationship, it is important to note that most of these statistics are gathered by white people (mostly male and heterosexual), and are supported by white money in a country that elevates white European values.

In fact, a variety of family structures and relationships have always been created more by the spirit of individuals than the governing morality of the social times. People on the fringe of the mainstream, such as musicians, artists, social activists and rebels, have always created their relationship life according to their own values and growing desires. The great diversity of cultures pouring into North America have all contributed to the ongoing evolution of relationship and family life. Native and indigenous cultures have expanded the idea of family as universal. We are all related.

Freedom of Divorce

The public outcry fearing the collapse of the nuclear family is not a modern phenomenon. The first divorce in North America took place in colonial Massachusetts in 1639. Glenda Riley found that divorce rates for the Massachusetts colony were quite high relative to the population rate. In 1730 divorce rates grew at a faster rate than the population.[6] As divorce laws became more lenient, divorce rates escalated, because more of the population had the opportunity to end unhappy unions. Throughout U.S. history a strong segment of the population has vehemently blamed divorce for all social ills.[7] Such an outcry reveals more about the history of marriage as an institution of control than about the possible demons divorce might let loose.

Initially established as a business arrangement for affluent families to secure their wealth, marriage has been meant to control relationship life; its sexist roots have been meant to keep women subservient. The institution of marriage has devalued independence and the single person. In the United States, it also carries the legacy of being forbidden to people of color. As a heterosexist institution, it limits and hence devalues love, the spiritual glue that holds unions together. However, marriage based on love is a relatively new concept. "Most Puritans believed that love developed after marriage rather than as a prerequisite to it. If love failed to grow, couples were expected to stay together, bonded by their cooperation as economic partners and parents."[8] In fact, it wasn't until the mid to late 1700s that women's divorce petitions began to complain about loveless unions. However, without "fault," divorce was not easily granted. Therefore, the consequences of adultery, impotence, cruelty and desertion became cause to separate loveless marriages.[9]

Divorce has always been with us: as an actual legal decree, which individuals used immediately once they had access, or as an experience that infiltrated relationship life. Legal ties or separations do not necessarily reflect relationship experience. Our personal and public histories are filled with loveless marriages that seem more like divorce than union. The fact is, relationships have always had their own spirit regardless of the laws and norms of the times.

Our relationships are caught between the dichotomy of the historical root of marriage as a practical institution and the spirit of love and magic that irresistibly draws us together. The former is predictable and the latter mysterious; each reflects a different viewpoint. Relationship is an arrangement, an agreement made by the mind to create a secure and stable life. This practical viewpoint is convinced that we can control and create our experience together and that our will can surpass any difficulty. It also reflects our desire for permanence and security. Another viewpoint is that relationship is an unpredictable journey connected to our dreams and personal growth and the spirit between us. One cannot will or create these dreams or lead the spirit, but can only follow the great mystery of our connections and separations. From this perspective the institutions of marriage and divorce have little meaning.

The Legacy of Fault

Many people in the process of divorce not only need help through the emotional loss and change of life that separation brings, but often feel depressed because they think of themselves as failures at relationship. It wasn't until 1970 that California became the first state to implement the revolutionary "no fault" divorce. By 1977 only three states retained an adversarial system of divorce.[10] It is quite astounding that in only seven years most of the states had made this radical change, discarding the centerpiece on which all previous divorces had been granted. People seemed all too ready to shed the legal legacy of blame and guilt central to ending their marital unions. And yet, why is it that decades later so many people feel that divorce is a sign of failure?

The law has freed us from fault, and yet the impulse to blame, assign guilt and drown in failure is still binding. Laws often emerge in reaction to or as an outgrowth of conflicting opinions, but only when those differences are given the chance to fully engage, and to process their interaction with great awareness, can the changes implicit in law become a living reality. Otherwise, our legal changes remain as dreams, waiting to be realized.

It was during the height of the sexual revolution, a decade before the advent of AIDS, that "no fault" divorce was introduced into law, marking the first legal intervention in divorce law since its inception. People wanted to leave the legacy of fault that had structured and created much of relationship life and interaction. As divorce rates escalated and marital affairs were brought out into the open, many reveled in newfound freedom and the joy of experience without responsibility. Breaking free from the moralistic holds on relationship, drunk on liberation, monogamy took a giant blow. However, monogamy itself is not the enemy; it is merely one vision of relationship. Even with the experimental atmosphere of the 60s and 70s, fault flourished. Sometimes only friends or therapists were privy to the inner workings of doubt and sense of failure. Other times, relationships cycled in the never-ending battle of accusation and blame, ending with regret and bitterness.

Any conflict must be addressed on a variety of interactional levels in order for sustainable change to occur.[11] Systemic and outer change cannot exist in isolation without addressing the levels of interaction that take place in our inner lives and play themselves out in our relationship dynamics. Therefore, even though the law might free us from fault, will our partner and the voices that populate our inner world be as forgiving? Sustainable systemic change can only occur when inner, relationship and community levels of focus are also addressed and transformed. Without such comprehensive dialogue, a new system has the unconscious potential of retaining something of the old one and thus becoming like it.

Relationship Revolution

The sexual revolution of the 60s and 70s challenged conventional relationship ideals. The free love movement supported people to have a variety of relationship experiences. I remember the mother of my first boyfriend asserting her viewpoint. "Young people should absolutely have sex before marriage. You need to know your partner sexually before you can make any long-term commitment." She was a radical mother; hers was the only house I knew where teenagers could have sex with her knowledge and blessing. She was smart; she knew she couldn't stop it and provided a place where at least she knew her kids were safe.

An air of revolution shook many households and families found themselves in the grips of a cultural war. Sides were drawn as free love flaunted itself in reaction to a controlling moralistic patriarchy steeped in the practical and puritanical values of old Europe. But what was to take its place? The orderly world of heterosexual monogamous marriage and family life was so convenient, so functional. Free love was the beginning of a dream, but of what? What was to replace the old order? As in many rebellions, the reactive side only knows that it is against the prevailing system; the seeds of discontent need gestation and unfolding to reveal a new vision of what is to come.

Where Are We at Fault?

Before we free ourselves from the chains of fault and explore a vision of relationship that isn't based on failing and succeeding, we might also ask if "fault" could bring us some significance or learning. Faced with an accusation or criticism, most of us defend against the judgment that we have done "wrong." The need to defend against a total devastation of our person escalates and we are unable to be open to our partner. Learning is not present, and for this we are all at fault. We have lost the viewpoint that relationships are a garden for growth. Most of us are at fault because we lack relationship skills; when conflict occurs we remain polarized and walk off in a self-righteous huff. But how can we do any better? Where can we learn the skills and feeling attitudes that are necessary when our relationships face challenges? In a world where most conflict escalates into war and enemies remain distant or hostile, we are all faced with the challenge of improving our relationship skills.

Unfolding the Dream of No Fault

Fault could not be as pervasive in our collective relationship consciousness if it were not for success. If there is success there must be failure and vice versa. Together success and failure create a philosophy based on a duality of experience, in which some experiences are rejected and others embraced. What worldview could replace the duality of success and failure, good and bad, or right and wrong? If we imagine a world in which no one way is "successful" to the detriment of all others what kind of world do we dream up?

The *I Ching*, the ancient spiritual text of Taoist thought, is generously sprinkled with the reminder, "no blame."[12] The popularity of Eastern thought and spiritual philosophy beyond the borders of Asia in the last few decades has had great appeal in part because it emphasizes inner development and the relativity of experience as opposed to the materialistic and concrete philosophy of right and wrong. The dreaming mind often leads us to cultures that are foreign to us in order to explore and create new experience.[13]

If experience is Tao or the way of nature, then all experience has the potential to be valuable in some way. There is no duality, but rather an emphasis on learning, which collapses an absolute duality. From this viewpoint, relationships can be seen as gardens to grow in.[14] Some gardens are populated with wild flowers, others have weeds or desert flowers, some are on hills and terraces, while others are in meadows. Each has its own terrain and foliage, its own unique character, available for our discovery. When the duality of success and failure motivates our relationships, we are bound to be searching for fault. When learning leads the way there is no blame.

One Love Forever = Success?

"Everyone thinks we are the perfect family. They look up to our marriage. We've been together for twenty years, have great kids. I feel like something is wrong with me. It is all I ever wanted and I feel like such a failure. Why can't I be happy?" Distraught, my client looks at me, berating herself for her misery, pleading to know why she isn't experiencing the success that everyone else around her projects onto her life. I hear such stories of lost love and the sense of doom and failure that follow daily. Just as often, I listen to the high dreams of those newly in love and the atmosphere of success and hopefulness that they carry. "This is it!" a client exclaims. "She is the one, the one I have been waiting for. All my other relationships were terrible; no one can hold a candle to her. This will be forever." He relaxes back into his chair, dreaming of eternal love.

This is a beautiful, powerful dream that propels many of us into our relationships. The experience of being together forever is a deep and transpersonal celebration of a bond beyond space and time. But what happens in the event that the relationship ends? Naturally, when we are dreaming of eternal love, divorce statistics or the rate at which people split up, do not usually enter our thoughts. If the relationship does end, what happens to our dream? Were we deluded, was our relationship a failure, will we ever meet anyone again? Should we give up on relationships all together?

One of the most deeply held relationship ideals is that we will fall in love with one person and live happily ever after. Some people have this experience, but many others do not. Most of us will have many relationships in our adult lives. As long as the epiphany of relationship life culminates in one "marriage"[15] in an adult life, many of us are bound to fail, and our divorces become statistics used to prove our family breakdowns. Although it is less common these days for an adult person to have one intimate relationship for life, it is still an ideal that many of us aspire to.

We can't yet be freed from fault unless we have a more fluid view of relationship, one that includes a variety of relationships and encourages our learning.

Relationship as a Garden for Growth

Why do we have relationships? Why are we drawn to them? Certainly we have them because we are a social species; we crave love and companionship and we need each other to survive. We also have relationships to grow. Most of us learn about ourselves and develop in interaction with others. We learn about love and intimacy and work through areas of ourselves that don't feel loved or loving. Our relationships help bring up patterns and experiences from earlier years or our family of origin for us to discover and explore. We learn about conflict and disagreement and difference. Relationships bring us to the borders of what we know about ourselves; they challenge us to stretch our identities and contact that which seems foreign. They reflect parts of us that we disavow and then can discover in ourselves. We learn about altered states and transpersonal experiences that emerge as we dream together and open up to new realms of experience.

Those of us coming of age in the 60s and 70s and thereafter had more cultural support to have a variety of intimate relationships. Most people in earlier generations married at young ages and remained together until death. Divorce was more unusual, and living together before marriage was very rare. It is different to fall in love at twenty than at forty or eighty. Different times in life also effect the kinds of relationships we have and how we come together.

Relationship Myths

Each relationship has its own spirit, its own learning, governed by our dreams, the unconscious glue that connects us. The Yaqui Indian shaman don Juan Matus claimed that power brought people together.[16] Author Carlos Castaneda describes how power selected him as don Juan's apprentice and created the relationship between them. This dreaming power creates relationships, draws individuals to channel certain experiences, brings different people together, and offers learning tasks. It is not just our will or intention that creates relationship. That is why we say that "relationships are made in heaven," or we thank the stars or the spirits for the people who have come into our lives. Or, we might feel upset or confused that we get into certain relationships, might feel that we repeat patterns and wonder why we are in such relationships. Either way we feel that something in our relationship life is out of our control. Something else creates both the awesome and the devastating experiences.

Arnold Mindell refers to this spiritual glue as a "relationship myth." Each relationship has a myth or a story that structures it and can be seen in the early dreams or memories of the couple.[17] For example, a heterosexual couple tell me their first memory. They met at a party and he was taken by how outgoing and friendly she was. He felt that she had an incredible exuberance and was fascinated by her. She noticed that he was sitting alone and felt drawn to him. She asked him to dance and he was very shy. They both giggle as they tell me how shy he was and how forward she was, and how it took quite a while before they had sex together. She remembered a dream in which she met a young doe in the forest. He recalled a dream from their early beginnings where she was taking him to a nightclub and when they arrived she told him they were to be the star performers. Working with this couple on these early dreams and memories revealed that they were joined by an extroverted and expressive spirit and also a very sensitive and shy one. A nightclub dancer and a doe were in relationship; the discovery and interaction between these two figures constitute their myth or story. Each of them is challenged to learn more about their own sensitivity and expressiveness and how these two parts interact together.

In another situation, two women had been together for many years and were having trouble, wondering if they should split up. They told me that they were great friends before they had become lovers. One of them had a dream that they were in ancient times and were leaders of a great tribe. They were given a task; one had to stay with the people and the other had to go into battle. Working with these women brought out their great friendship and the inevitable differences and tasks that they had in the world. They both could see that the romantic partnership was not the essential thing that held them together, but a deeper friendship and community work. They parted in tears but knew the direction that they were going was the right path.

The perspective of a myth gives a learning emphasis to relationship. In the above example, the women did not split up because "they couldn't make it work" or because one of them was wrong or insufficient. They didn't part in blame and accusation, but each learned something of their own nature and of the deeper connection or myth between them. Although they suffered the grief of loss and change in their relationship, they also felt the relief and personal enrichment that comes from learning and following the dreaming that creates our relationships.

Relationships and Dreaming

Our relationship culture has changed quite a bit in the last decades; my grandmother, who divorced twice in the 1930s and 40s, felt great shame as she tried to hide her divorces and fled from neighborhoods that knew her too well. High divorce rates come as no surprise to me and I don't feel badly about the numbers of couples who end their unions. I don't think it reflects badly on our society and means that the nuclear family is breaking down, nor do I feel we are not as faithful as we once were.

Vows before God, sworn in holy matrimony, promises of love forever exchanged in precious moments, do not seem to keep us together till death do us part nor do they keep us all faithful. Many of us search for the faithful partner, imagining that we simply need to find a person with enough strength, willpower, and honesty. But faith is not cultivated by good intentions alone. It breaks down when it is tied to moral codes or the intentions of an unmoving identity. We are changing beings and our dream life will always remind us of this. Dreaming tells us that we truly are everything; we are awesome, unpredictable beings and our lines of certainty will always be challenged. From this perspective we can only be truly faithful to the dreaming process that continually creates our relationships.

I expect high divorce and separation rates because I expect people to want to learn as much as they can in this lifetime. Therefore, many of us will end relationships when we develop outside of the parameters of our unions or complete the myths that have joined us. Many of us will realize that we have been in relationship with individuals who resemble parental figures from our childhood; immersed in these deep patterns, we have the chance to learn and react and grow in ways that were not possible when we were younger. These relationships are crucial in helping us to complete old patterns and create new ones. There is no blame here; so many of our earliest relationships unearth these skeletons that we might even expect and welcome it. Some couples have a myth that will hold them together beyond the learning of these familiar patterns. Most of us will not, and we will move on in our relationship journey where other dreams and learning tasks will connect us to other people.

Shedding the shame of divorce, we are in the midst of relationship revolution. Divorce has become more common as people realize that maintaining their unions for economics, children, family ideals or social convention is not enough. Relationship that thrives and sustains itself must be based on the core of our dreaming process, the intangible lines of learning that connect, challenge and further our growth. From this perspective, we survey our relationship history and can see the value in our own development, even in the midst of pain. This is the revolution that will replace the legacy of fault.

Relationship life is coming out of the closet as a place to discover ourselves—a great arena for personal and social exploration. Relationship based on dreaming means that our contacts and families are not created by moral codes but by shared ideals and myths. Family life is expanding and flourishing. The African American concept of appropriation is the cornerstone of many family units. Many of us experience ourselves as members of a tribe, a global community modeled after indigenous family structures. Furthermore, relationship has become the primary vehicle for us to learn more about "others." As the world has grown smaller, many of us will create family with people from radically different cultures, countries, races, and backgrounds from our own. Cultures that might have remained unknown or forbidden to us become very real in the intimacy of love and family. For many of us, relationship is worldwork; our interracial and cultural unions, extended families and same gender relationships challenge society's view of love and family. Could it be that the great dream that propels such diversity is really a teacher of love and learning, revealing the inescapable web of dreaming that connects us all in a world community?

End Notes

[1] Andrew Billingsley, *Climbing Jacob's Ladder: The Enduring Legacy of African-American Families* (NY: Simon and Schuster, 1992).
[2] Billingsley 334
[3] Billingsley 28.
[4] Billingsley 31.
[5] Glenda Riley, *Divorce: An American Tradition* (NY: Oxford University Press, 1991) 14.
[6] Riley 17.
[7] Riley 17.
[8] Riley 16.
[9] Riley 16.
[10] Riley 163.
[11] In March of 1998 Drs. Arnold and Amy Mindell gave a training seminar on worldwork on the Oregon coast. Arnold Mindell spoke about the need for noting the different levels of interaction that occur during group process: systemic, inner work, relationship interactions and group interactions. When each level of interaction is completely processed, change happens fluidly on all levels.

[12] *I Ching or Book of Changes,* trans. Richard Wilhelm (London: Routledge and Kegan Paul, 1951).

[13] See my dissertation "Emerging World Views: Cultural Transformation in Process Oriented Psychology," Union Institute, 1989, for discussion and examples of how our dreaming takes us into cultures that are foreign to our identities in order to create and elicit new patterns for experience

[14] I am grateful to Arny Mindell for this viewpoint that is central to process work and can be noted in his approach to relationships in *The Dreambody in Relationship.*

[15] I put the word "marriage" in quotation marks here to include couples who have strong unions; the word marriage could describe their relationship, however they have not been legally married. Gay couples cannot legally marry and many heterosexual couples do not marry for a variety of reasons, some of them in protest against the discriminatory legacy that marriage has carried.

[16] Carlos Castaneda, *Journey to Ixtlan; Tales of Power* (NY: Simon and Schuster, 1972, 1974).

[17] Early dreams and memories of all beginnings reveal a mythic dreaming story. Mindell drew on Jung's research into childhood dreams that demonstrated that the first dreams and nightmares that we remember from childhood are blueprints for our life, revealing major life tasks and learnings that accompany us throughout our life. Many of these dreams are transpersonal, pieces of experience that are personal and also beyond personal experience connecting us to a larger life task.

For more in-depth discussion on relationship myths and working with relationships, see Arnold Mindell, *The Dreambody in Relationships.*

Falling in Love

I.

I awake this morning and you are not beside me. Yet I stir as if you had reached for me, pulled me close into the soft, strong curves and warmth of your body. I feel the sheets against my skin in a way that I usually don't. My hands have become your hands as they slowly travel down my smooth sides, feeling the movement of muscle and bone, pausing to hold the arc of my hip, sliding to grab velvety rounds.

I feel different to myself. The subtle self-hatred and familiar disgust of collective comparison is absent. I don't know myself without it. I am swept away not only by a new love, but by my own eagerness to feel myself. I curiously explore my body with the enthusiasm and joy of a new lover.

I dress for you. My eyes scan my underwear drawer and immediately fix on the lacy, white pair that make me feel so sexy. I know you will joyfully discover them later this evening. As I ease into them I appreciate the line of hip and waist, how the thin satin straps sit just right on my bones. I am aware of how clothing hangs on my frame; how jeans hug my flesh as if I am held by your arms.

I catch glimpses of myself in the mirror, getting out of the shower, in restaurant bathrooms, in store windows, and find myself surprised that I take a second look. You—you are the second look, or maybe the original look that I forgot long ago. The first look belongs to the culture that cemented my identity, formed and molded me until my perceptions of myself automatically mirrored the cultural ideals around me. I am a product of a world that worships homogeneity and overlooks the precious beauty of individual nature.

But you are now everywhere, flooding my awareness; warm waters rush over me and the first world is gone. Your eyes follow me with the attention of a god and the lust of a lion. You are perceiving me, creating me anew.

Growing up, I could never imagine a god who smiled. God seemed so serious in Judeo-Christian culture, created in man's image, completely of this world and involved in the everyday travails of his people. It wasn't until I saw pictures and sculptures of smiling Buddhas and ecstatic Hindu gods and goddesses that I knew God could smile. I knew then that God was not entirely of the human culture we all strive to maintain, but could leap with joy and ecstasy into other worlds—unbound and free, everywhere and nowhere. Now—when I look at you looking into me—I know what God looks like smiling. And I know that you know God is smiling back.

II.

I saw you in a wild erotic ecstasy and woke screaming in the night. Then I had to laugh. This was a nightmare? What scared me so? Your head thrown back, hair floating in mid-air, suspended, eyes crazy with lust and self-absorption, a dervish whirling through space and time, where nothing else exists but the universe.

In a few hours I would be lying under the surgeon's knife to have a fibroid adenoma removed from my breast. The circle of friends who had come to see me off tucked me into a cozy bed at a wonderful clinic that looked like a Victorian home. When the anesthesia took me I felt confident that the small lump in my breast was not dangerous and I said goodbye to wonderful friends who would be there to greet me in an hour. I drifted into another world from the anesthesia, enjoying the altered state.

This time I did not scream when I woke up. I was ecstatic. Eyes closed, I could hear voices around me. A nurse was trying to stir me, to bring me back to this world. I heard her say that everything went well and the lump was indeed what they had thought, a fibroid adenoma. I was in no hurry to come back. I already knew what was being told to me. I felt pulled into my experience and let myself go more deeply into it. The nurse must have sensed that my friends were comfortable with such states as they gathered around the bed, eager to relate to me where I was, and she left us alone.

You were the one who kissed me. I was in an exquisite state, deeply happy, squirming with delight. I watched myself savor every movement and feeling. Everything felt so delicious. Warm legs sliding on slightly cool sheets, arms wrapped around myself, hands gently greeting the hollows of my cheeks, re-discovering the features of my face. I lay in a bed of silk, a bundle of sensual delight. Such tender feelings demanded to be shared and I watched myself daringly reach to those around me. The regulated world of relationship borders and comfort zones had no appeal to me; something else led me to ask for a kiss.

I felt the discomfort in the room. Although I couldn't open my eyes, I could see the nervous looks, the hesitations, the silent sorting of the complicated relationship dynamics amongst us. It was you, the person who knew me least, who felt most drawn and comfortable to touch your sweet lips to mine. Again and again, delicate kisses left me trembling. Like a baby bird waiting for an early morning feeding, my mouth reached for you. Like the earth awaiting the first rays of sun, I bathed in your warmth. I felt I was coming home.

Later you told me that there was no way for you to resist me. You could never have left such a special state unmet. I knew then that we shared a similar longing for deep states and ecstatic experiences, that ordinary life paled in comparison.

Then and now, I love to watch you throw yourself to the winds of experience, let them take you and ride you. I too am possessed by their callings, willing to leave what I know. I am no longer afraid.

III.

My basketball buddies tease me as I stumble onto the court, obviously tired, and totally miss the rim of a shot that I usually easily make. "Hey, what were you up to last night?" someone asks provocatively. I feel my cheeks redden. I smile shyly, put my head down, and run off after the ball. "Give her a few months, the honeymoon will soon be over!" I shrug off their comments, hold onto the warmth inside, and try to find my shot again.

My environment seems just as consumed by my new love as I am. I had forgotten about the powerful effects falling in love can stimulate. A new relationship is like nectar for the bees, a sweet altered state that irresistibly attracts. People innocently ask me about you and tell me I look great. They smile knowingly as if we were sharing this great intimate secret. I think we are.

"The honeymoon will soon be over." That comment rings in my head, like a mantra everyone seems to agree to. The honeymoon refers to the early blissful stages of relationship where love, sex and new intimacy color everything. Ordinary reality freezes itself and holds little interest. The world waits on the sidelines, applauding the glow of love and dreaming of its own. It calls, pulls and hypnotizes us into thinking that our experiences are limited and that the "real world" will sooner or later dominate our consciousness once again.

Consensus reality tells me that such bliss doesn't last. I become stubborn against this belief and hold on as tightly as a starved child to her last crust of bread. I am hungry to believe that relationship is an exciting and evolving experience. That means everything evolves and changes, not only the first desires of lust, but also everyday existence. Too often relationship becomes synonymous with the doings of everyday reality as we establish ourselves as long-term couples.

When I was sixteen I could not conceive of getting married. Relationships around me seemed stagnant and dull. Where was the passion and romance, except in the movies? At that age, I projected all these doubts onto monogamous relationships. I thought, like the culture around me, that intimate relationships are only meant to create families, offer security and a sense of home and stability.

The constant joy of discovery makes early love so numinous. We "fall" in love because we are knocked off balance; our stable sense of ourselves crumbles as new experiences come to birth. We yearn to be moved, to change and grow. At the same time, many of us long for home and security, which might be a new experience as well. Yet with time, we all seem to develop a relationship culture, a mini-culture with its own style and flavor, a coupling that is known and more or less predictable.

We expect certain behaviors and give predictable responses. We get the sense that we know each other. And we do, in part. But knowing someone else, or ourselves for that matter, is not a finite accomplishment. How can anyone possibly know me when my own life is a mystery, a continual discovery of my evolving self? Relationship offers an eternal pool of discovery which never dries up as long as we follow the unknown, uncomfortable and surprising elements in our interactions and our dreams. These unfamiliar moments hold the potential for continual growth. Too often we forget this after the glow of new love fades. I also like the predictable world. I like home, coming into warm arms I know will receive me. And I like the edge of the unknown, the thrilling and uncomfortable spot that teases me into exploring new parts of myself.

As I lie beside you, I wonder what you will bring out of me today. I not only anticipate your touch, but your loving focus that unearths central aspects of my being. You look at me greedily and I notice my sudden shyness, followed by the discomfort of being off familiar ground. Instead of making myself more comfortable and quickly moving off that spot, I explore my uneasiness. I go more deeply into my shy feelings, let my head drop to my chest and allow my shoulders to curl. A small smile warms my face and a rainbow of tenderness expands across my chest. "You make me feel like a daisy," I whisper. Strong, sure arms hold me tighter. I am blushing like a newborn flower, slightly self-conscious as I slowly open my delicate petals for you to see. Your greed grows as hips roll over dampened fields like thunder while I hold on, swaying in the wind. You too are embracing something new. I watch you follow and unfold new sensations. I have never known this strength in you, this mountain, sure and steady, weathered and wise. A daisy melts in your arms, grateful for how love lures us into self-discovery and unknown worlds.

Falling in love is not only an early stage of relationship. It is a powerful altered state that serves as a possible pattern for living life, for following and discovering what is unknown and wanting to be born. Living life as a turn-on means that we are attracted not only by what is known and familiar but by that which is distracting and off balance, constantly challenging us to discover new and unknown worlds. Life becomes a total attraction, sexy, as consuming and fascinating as new love. We want to hold onto our honeymoons in an attempt to hold this precious state of discovery and magic, to ward off the complacency of consensus reality.

Therefore, couples in love attract and stimulate the environment. We are drawn to these couples because we want to get close to this state in ourselves and in our relationships. We stare at lovers and remember states in the past or long for experiences in the future. We dream of the high states we have always yearned for. We want to be opened, discovered and valued.

Love is a gift, a privilege that is often taken for granted, and therefore, a state that also constellates jealousy. Many of us suffer silently, ashamed of our jealousy, embarrassed to admit our secret longings for intimacy. However, jealousy is a calling—an awakening of a hunger that gnaws and tugs at us until it is satisfied. Its intensity reflects our desperation for inspiration and the drive to pursue our highest ideals in relationship. In fact, jealousy could be our greatest ally, alerting us to some of our deepest desires.

I don't think honeymoons need to end. They can expand endlessly as we hunger for the continual desire to be unfolded and constantly discovered.

Beyond Tolerance[1]

Culture and Sexuality

When the female rap group, Salt n' Pepa, came out with the hit tune "Let's Talk about Sex," the infectious beat possessed me and the lyrics relentlessly sang in my head.[2] I also heard the message and was elated that the simple words and catchy tune would possess millions of others. We don't talk enough about sex, especially publicly. In fact, Salt n' Pepa feared that their hit song would be censored and not given radio time. Talking about sex brings sexuality itself out of the closet, and encourages our growth as sexual beings.

I like this song even though the lyrics are exclusively heterosexual. They have to be. The song could never have made it to mainstream popularity if the lyrics were more inclusive or the musicians were out as gay, lesbian or bisexual. It would be judged as "too sexual," "too extreme," or "obscene" because the sexual minority community are open slates for sexual and "deviant" projections. When popular gay musicians do sing about love and sexuality, the words are often in code. For example, k.d. lang and Melissa Etheridge rarely, if ever, use direct female pronouns in their lyrics or love songs. Nor does Elton John use direct male pronouns in his love songs. You might recall the big hit tune YMCA by the Village People, which is about gay male cruising at the Y, but this was totally unknown to the general public. In fact, this song enjoyed a big revival at the 1996 Olympics in Atlanta when it was played over and over at various sporting events. Mainstream USA rocked out in the stands mouthing the refrain. I doubt they knew what they were singing about.

Much of the hoopla and controversy around gay sexuality has little to do with same sex relationships; rather, it is a reflection of mainstream culture trying to get along with being sexual. We have a problem with sex, which is reflected in how we split off aspects of our sexuality and project them onto marginalized groups. One might notice that some aspect of sexual behavior is often used to further marginalize most minority groups. Common statements you might have heard include: "they do it like rabbits, they have big penises, they are hot lovers, they are whores, sluts, they'll do it with anything that moves, one is never enough for those people, they can really move, they molest children, they always have someone on the side, they want it both ways." For example, we in the mainstream vicariously enjoy the two black women who make up the team of Salt n' Pepa. The mainstream allows and needs and uses African Americans (as well as other marginalized groups) to carry sexual projections and at the same time chastises them for it.

The more we all develop and further ourselves as sexual beings, the fewer sexual projections we will have onto various groups of people, and the less attack there will be on the sexual minority community.

The mainstream treats gay sexuality as an aberration that can be changed. To even suggest that someone can change their loving, the core of self-expression and one of the most mysterious aspects of relationship, shows very little experience in matters of love. Love, intimacy and sexual feelings are not cognitive processes. Therefore, when the mainstream suggests behavioral changes, this says little about the sexual minority community, but it does say a lot about our culture—our lack of development around matters of love, sex and feeling.

Those of us who identify as gay, lesbian or bisexual might keep this in mind when we interact with people who feel uncomfortable or critical around our sexuality. Oftentimes we interact with our families and culture with the hope they will accept us. However, the emphasis is too often on *us*. We must adapt ourselves, plead for inclusion, and adjust our behavior so others feel comfortable. The deeper changes happen when our families and communities connect inwardly with their own most intimate feelings and have an experience of what it is like to be us, to even know that in some sense they *are* us.

My parents took the news of my first female lover pretty hard. The gloomy mood hung over our relationship for many years. I still remember one particular conversation I had with my mother during that time. She was talking about the difficulty and strain in her relationships with friends and family members who assumed that I was straight. They would ask her if I had met a man yet and when I was going to get married. My mother would change the subject or lie and portray me as a career woman with little time for relationships.

I watched my mother from across the table. Her tense posture and clipped sentences revealed her anger at me for having put her in this situation. Beneath the chilly atmosphere I saw her panic and discomfort and pain. I suddenly realized that she was the "lesbian." She looked like me and everyone else I know who at one time or another fears being different. I told her that until she developed the inner strength and compassion to stand up proudly as a unique woman and mother in her peer group she would never be able to value me. I explained to her that "lesbian" is a role that anyone can have in a given moment. When I am with her, I am the lesbian, the one in the minority position, and she is the majority culture. When I am gone and she is with her friends or parents, she is the lesbian, the one standing alone against mainstream culture. In those moments when she is uncomfortable, insecure or terrified to speak about her daughter's relationship life, she is experiencing what every person in the sexual minority community experiences at one time or another.

The Tyranny of Mainstream Comfort

My partner and I were at our local gym when the owner approached us in the locker room. "I need to tell you that one of our members was very uncomfortable with the affection between you. This type of behavior is not appropriate." Shock and fury burned through my body while my mind raced backwards, trying to remember what possible behavior could have been so inappropriate and forbidden.

I had arrived at the gym earlier and Renata met me on her way home from work just as I was finishing my workout. I was thrilled to see her walk in the door and we greeted each other with a kiss. As we stood at the leg press, I in my sweats, she in her coat, we briefly discussed our day, who would stop at the store on the way home, and when we would meet for dinner—just the common behavior any couple who lived together would display. However, we were happy. I do remember gazing at her and smiling with happiness, an obvious air of intimacy between us.

I think the owner of the gym expected us to shrivel up and walk away, accepting our fate as second class citizens and yielding to the predominant consensus that kept gay couples in constant check. I tried to keep my cool, reminding myself that my deeper goals were transformation even though hurt and anger pulsed violently throughout my body.

"I have seen heterosexual couples greet each other in a similar fashion, is this also forbidden? Is it all affection that you are against or just homosexual affection?" The owner seemed taken aback at being challenged so directly. She looked down and shuffled her feet. "No, I don't think that type of behavior is appropriate in public for heterosexual or homosexual couples." I asked her what kind of behavior we were talking about, particularly since the behavior in question was visible between heterosexual couples daily in the gym. "Since I didn't actually see what you did, it sounds like I would have no problem with that kind of greeting." She began to back down, but statements that I am sure she intended as harmless stumbled out of her mouth and inflamed me more.

"We have many lesbian members and we have never had this kind of problem before." The hairs on my spine stood at attention as happens whenever my opinions, perceptions or behavior are dismissed as being an exception. Such statements are meant to make one feel foolish and insignificant and offer a convenient out for anyone in power to be let off the hook. This is one way the majority culture unconsciously uses its powers to keep those who are different silent and in their place. It is humiliating and terrifying to be the "only one."

"You know not everyone is comfortable with homosexuality," she continued. I couldn't believe this one. She was telling this to us! Could she be naïve enough to think that we were unaware of the majority culture we were living in, how every day we had to deal with a culture that does not include us due to its discomfort?

"At the moment I feel very uncomfortable being a member at your club. Does my discomfort have less value than the member who complained about us?" "Of course not," she said. I continued and stated the obvious, that some people are uncomfortable around indigenous people, white people, black people, people with accented English, rich and powerful people, poor people, obese and anorexic people, disabled and disfigured people. My list could obviously go on. I was making a point and I wanted to know whose comfort was most important. I was sick and tired of living in a world where majority comfort prevailed at everyone else's expense.

I told her I was not interested in supporting a society that only keeps the majority comfortable. In my mind this is a crucial problem. Whenever the mainstream feels uncomfortable, it feels an undeniable right to adjust the behavior and rights of everyone else so it can remain comfortable. Meanwhile, all of those who are outside of mainstream culture continually deal with social, financial and emotional discomfort due to this unconscious entitlement of the majority culture.

I love being comfortable as much as the next person, yet we miss important experiences in our discomfort. When we are taken out of our comfort zone, the moment is ripe for new experience and growth. We often think that raising our children with little hardship and maximum comfort is ideal. I share this belief in part; I don't like to see anyone suffer, particularly children. And yet, a little discomfort, challenge and diversity creates character and depth.

Some years ago I was sitting on an airplane next to a young, white heterosexual couple. Since I had been out of the country for a few weeks I asked them who had won the women's NCAA basketball championship. Little did I know I was to engage in a huge dialogue around racism. In his response, the man referred to the "colored" girls who played basketball. I was outraged and wondered how I was going to engage with his racism. "How is it that in 1997 you are still calling African American women colored?" I asked him. He was obviously embarrassed and a long dialogue around racism ensued. Suddenly, he asked me if I believed in interracial marriage. I told him that I celebrated love wherever it occurred, that it was a mysterious and beautiful happening. He pursued the issue more deeply, "Well, how do you think it is for the children of interracial marriages? This does not seem to be good for the children."

I told him that when I look at the children from homes of two heterosexual parents of the same religion and race, I don't think these children are necessarily better people. They might have more worldly opportunities and they might be more comfortable fitting into mainstream society, but I don't see this as better. He looked at me totally bewildered. I continued. "In fact, I often think that the special challenges those children have, which at times are uncomfortable, create character and compassion in children. Such children tend to feel more comfortable in a variety of situations, are perhaps more open-hearted to a greater diversity of people, and have a depth of feeling and experience that might be less developed in other children." He gave that some thought and got up to use the toilet. When he came back I had a sense that something in our conversation had penetrated his thinking. He seemed relaxed but alert and engaged me in further conversation.

The most conspicuous comfort of the mainstream is that it need only embrace one position. It can remain one-sided because the culture is a mirror of itself. However, this is naïve. Culture is extraordinarily diverse, and if we don't raise our children with an openness to its diversity, we do not prepare our children for the world they will be living in. In such a world both comfort and discomfort would be shared and the value of discomfort would be appreciated. Discomfort means we are forced into a new realm; it is time to learn and open up, expand ourselves, connect with others, and be enriched by experiences that we otherwise would not have.

Sexuality as a Fluid Process

Sexuality, like all behavior and experience, is a fluid and unpredictable process. Too often we freeze sexual experience. Not only do we freeze into a sexual identity, but we freeze out spontaneous experience and the changing elements in our relationships. We find what is comfortable and we stay there. We split off sexual fantasies and experiences that seem strange, and we keep all kinds of unknown experience in our relationships at bay. We become settled; we create a relationship culture, a way of being, interacting, living, and loving.

Relationship cultures are important. They give us the feeling of home, a place where we can relax and feel that life is more or less predictable in a forever-changing universe. While we enjoy this comfort, we might consider exploring what is unknown, outside our own "mainstream culture," no matter what kind of relationship we have. Working at the borders of our known worlds means picking up unintentional and dream-like experiences that are constantly present. The unknown world of our dreams presents itself in all of the spontaneous body signals, fantasies, movements and sounds as well as in the disturbing and strange experiences that we encounter in relationship and the world.[3]

Because we have little control of our physical and sexual experiences, sexuality is an area where new and unknown elements of ourselves and our relationships emerge. The mind or identity does not reign, although it tries to. The identity tries to create the kinds of sexual encounters it wants, it tries to will itself to turn on or off, it tries to block out certain fantasies or thought patterns and to introduce others, it has ideas about how sex should be and when and how often sex should happen. When the identity's power does not prevail we might avoid sex, or we might feel that there is something wrong with us, or perhaps we declare that we have a "sexual problem" and go to a therapist. An alternative is to think that something new and unknown is disturbing our own "mainstream" or comfortable way of relating. In its most basic definition, this is what dreaming is. Dreaming is the unknown coming into being. When we sleep and our intention is no longer ours, dreams bring us into other worlds. These unknown worlds also occur in waking states in the form of experience that is outside of our intentions.[4]

The world of sexuality will not be tamed and unknown parts of ourselves find fertile ground irrespective of sexual identity, or of any identity at all. In fact, oftentimes it is our sexual identity that inhibits us from exploring and learning more about ourselves and our relationships.

I remember working with a gay man who kept unconsciously brushing up against my breast. In addition, when he would greet me or hug me his hand was a little too close to my breast for my own natural comfort. I took this as a signal from the dreaming world trying to emerge, something for us to discover.[5]

When I brought it to his attention, he was terribly embarrassed and couldn't understand how he, as a gay man, would be touching my breast. I assured him that he could still be a gay man, but it might be interesting to explore why his body kept gravitating towards my breasts. I made him feel at home, and he was open to exploring how these unconscious signals might be important. I encouraged him to fantasize what it might be like to touch my breast. In his fantasy he was drawn to my nipples. He imagined them to be perky and excited. Normally shy, in his fantasy he would grab my nipple, the excitement, he said. He then revealed that he didn't really know how to be as intimate as he sometimes felt with people. He experienced all of his relationships as lacking a certain intimacy or excitement, remaining too superficial. Inadvertently, in his body signal with me, he was trying to bring in this excitement and get closer. Our work continued as I encouraged him to pursue what excited and interested him in all of his relationships. That would be the meaning of going right for the nipple!

I remember a "straight" couple who came to see me because they were having troubles sexually. They were very nervous as he quietly stated that he had been having some dreams about being sexual with men and found himself having homosexual fantasies. He had never had sex with a man before and was very nervous about his feelings. His wife said she felt very insecure and afraid he would leave her. Understanding sexuality as a fluid process in which our intentions are sometimes disturbed by a variety of relationship signals, I suggested we explore it together.

I asked him what he imagined it would be like to sleep with a man. He was shy, but imagined an erect penis and a hard, muscular body. As he described his fantasy, his wife sat back against the wall; she seemed to retreat and looked depressed. I asked her what she was experiencing and she said it made her feel worthless. He then became very animated and said that that was the problem. She always felt worthless and defeated—he wanted her to be stronger. He felt that she was never really there. She was always disappearing in defeat, feeling badly about herself. However, he shared this experience; he too got defeated and didn't react strongly in the system between them.

I encouraged him to feel in his whole body the experience of an erect penis and hard body. He stood up and puffed out his chest and tensed his muscles. She perked up and smiled at him. I supported him to go a step further by bringing this body experience into movement. He began to strut across the room, powerfully dancing and thrusting his body. She was totally fascinated and I suggested that she follow her fascination and join him in the movement. The two engaged in a movement dance, bumping and stomping and strutting their powers. They laughed and embraced, enjoying a new kind of contact. It was beautiful. They both needed the quality of that strength, insistence and force. This was the great teaching behind his fantasies of sleeping with a man.

This process might bring up many questions about sexual identity. One might assert that he is gay and should leave his wife. Someone else might say that he is bisexual and another would insist he is straight and needs to integrate his projections onto gay sex in his marriage. As a therapist who follows nature, my focus is on unfolding the process of the couple and not determining their sexual identity. This couple wanted to stay together, so we emphasized their learning and development as a unit. At another point in time this might change. The point is not the gender of the person you sleep with; more important is picking up the process that is trying to occur.

There is no one way to explore ourselves sexually or in relationship, and there are many factors to feel into and consider and unfold. It takes a great deal of sensitivity and openness to continually unfold and experience the fluidity of our dreaming process in relationship and sexuality.

It is dangerous and frightening for many of us to consider that our sexual identities are not as solid as we had hoped. Generally, any attempt to discover what is unknown is a threat to our identity. In matters of sexuality, this fear seems to be doubly amplified.

Sometimes the only way we are able to explore a "forbidden" sexual experience is by fighting against it. I have often wondered about the amount of time many anti-gay activists spend immersed in gay literature. Some years ago I was in a popular gay bookstore in Washington D.C., engaged in a conversation with one of the clerks. He told me that one of their best customers was a conservative, fundamentalist, anti-gay activist who spent thousands of dollars each month at their bookstore and numerous hours each week perusing the shelves. It is ironic that someone who is so repulsed by gay sexuality spends so much time consumed by it. Yet it is dangerous for him to consider that being gay might be a part of who he is. He can only experience that part of himself vicariously through his research for the religious right. Such disavowed experiences are attempts for us to experience our wholeness. I can only imagine this man's dream life!

A Note of Caution

Suggesting that sexuality is a fluid experience for those in the sexual minority community is a sensitive and complicated issue. If you are part of a disavowed group and your very existence is threatened or your rights are limited, the culture presses you into the position of having to take a definitive stand in regard to your identity. If there are no role models for you and the culture is relatively devoid of your presence, you must make yourself known and insist on your identity. When you are fighting for your life you must strongly assert that you exist. If you waiver by being open to all the possibilities of your sexual self, the mainstream can dismiss you, marginalize you and insist that you can change, insist that you have a choice. Furthermore, the majority culture will then use one individual experience as proof to deny the validity of all gay relationships.

Therefore, the seeming lack of fluidity on the part of the sexual minority community and much of its insistence to have a strong and unwavering sexual identity is in part created by the majority culture's dismissal. This insistence is dreamt up, meaning that gay people are forced into the position of insisting on themselves, of creating an absolute and unmoving identity because they must fight for their existence on a daily basis. Dreaming up happens when we as individuals or groups become invariably one-sided and deny a part of ourselves. Far from vanishing, this part aspires towards wholeness, and becomes dream material, irrepressible and alive in our dreams and body signals. In this case, when the majority culture insists on heterosexuality as the norm and denies gay sexuality, the role of the homosexual must stand for itself all the more adamantly. The more rigid and one-dimensional the individual or cultural identity, the more dream material that is disavowed and the greater the need for the disavowed role to stand its ground.[6]

These dynamics must be appreciated and understood when approaching the gay community with the issue of sexual identity, an issue that demands the utmost respect and sensitivity. For a community that has been so hurt and judged, questioning and exploring sexual identity can seem like another judgment. This is why there is so much conflict around sexual identity even within the sexual minority community. It is a threat to explore an aspect of ourselves that we have had to fight so hard to maintain. However, we must. What about the woman who was married to a man for twenty years and then falls in love with a woman? What is she? How about the lesbian who after many years of being deeply involved with the lesbian community falls in love with a man? What about the man who is married to a woman but is also having relationships with men? What are these people?

When these changes occur our solid world of identity is shaken. Often the individual feels pressed to identify with his present experience and make an identity out of it, disregarding his past. For instance, the man who left his wife and three kids now tells everyone he is gay and always was. Or a woman who had lesbian relationships in her youth and then married a man explains away her early experiences as a phase. Cultural reactions also influence our identity. The mainstream acceptance of heterosexual relationships makes it easier to deny our gay histories. Gay culture wields great influential power as well. For example, a woman with a history of lesbian relationships and strong ties to the lesbian community is now intimately involved with a man. She tells everyone she is a lesbian insofar as she feels deeply connected to her lesbian self and the lesbian community, but many in the lesbian community reject her.

Without a fluid view of sexuality and relationships we may discount our experiences. Ex-partners struggle with this issue, trying not only to grapple with the loss of relationship, but with the change in sexual identity. For example, the woman who was left after fifteen years of marriage to a man now tries to comprehend her ex-husband's gay identity. "Does this mean my marriage was a sham?" she wonders. She dissects the entire marriage, trying to find the clues that would have led her to discover earlier her husband's "hidden" identity. She feels betrayed and hurt. She wonders if he ever loved her and how to view the man and the marriage that she was devoted to.

It is true that many people who have had long-term heterosexual relationships and find themselves involved in homosexual ones later in life assert that they have always been gay. Due to the homophobic culture we live in, such people found themselves in straight relationships trying to live a life that culture accepted. Only when they were stronger, had other influences and support systems, or met someone who knocked them off their feet were they able to engage in gay relationships. However, there are also a great number of individuals who felt free to enter the kinds of relationships that moved them. Furthermore, we must remember that when we evaluate our past relationships our viewpoint has changed. We have to remember what it was like when we were in them. The relationship we have at twenty is different than the one we have at forty or sixty; our growth in relationships and our development as sexual beings changes over time regardless of the gender of the person we are sleeping with.

In 1997, JoAnn Loulan, a well-known lesbian public speaker, sex therapist, author, and performer, whose one-woman shows were a sexual inspiration for many lesbians, announced in gay newspapers across the United States that she had fallen in love with a man. The reaction in my local Portland gay bi-monthly was electric and controversial.[7] A sensitive nerve had been touched and the newspaper became a forum for fascinating and explosive dialogue. The discussion polarized itself around two voices. One voice felt betrayed and hurt and mourned the loss of an old time advocate. This position took this perceived loss as a personal affront: "How could you do this to us?" they wrote in desperation. Another voice supported the woman to love whomever she wanted and reproached the others for their narrow-minded reactions.

After some months of dialogue, Loulan responded in an editorial in our local paper. She valued both positions, spoke of her personal struggles and declared that she still considered herself a lesbian. In closing she quoted an editorial in a lesbian and gay North Carolina paper that addresses the fluid nature of sexuality.

> [Loulan] has done the unforgivable. She has shown us that sexuality isn't static and, therefore, that there are few certainties in life. She has jeopardized many of her friendships and the goodwill of the lesbian community in the process, a stressful state of affairs to be sure. What if she had denied her feelings for this man for the sake of our community? Wouldn't that be a terrible betrayal, too?[8]

I bring this example out of the closet and into public view because this exciting dialogue needs to happen. Hiding from and fearing this discussion in an attempt to remain secure only makes us more vulnerable and unprepared. Exploration opens us up, offers us more flexibility, and frees us from having to keep our guard up. We need to explore the deeper needs we have in creating identity, our fears and uncertainties, and the role the culture has in polarizing us and creating absolute and unmoving identities. We also need to know that this exploration does not invalidate our relationships or our sexual preferences. Furthermore, the sexual minority community must be careful that we do not unconsciously become the inflexible and unmoving majority that is oppressive to us all.

Learning Together

This essay emerged from a lecture presented at the Process Work Center of Portland. During this lecture the question of exploring sexual identity created quite a stir, as it did when it arose in the local Portland gay newspaper. I have included some of this discussion as an example of the diversity of opinion that emerges through dialogue. I have taken some liberty in editing so that the discussion flows more easily, and names have been changed to protect confidentiality.

Ralph: I want to make a point on the example about the couple who worked on the man's homosexual fantasies. By doing that work their whole perspective around gay sexuality can change as they have an experience of gay sexuality in their relationship. If they as a mainstream couple have that experience, it means their projections onto gay couples are going to change.

Dawn: That's a good point. I didn't know their views about homosexuality or whether they were homophobic. I didn't work with the couple on a social level, but focused on their individual experience and fantasy of what gay sex would be like. However, I agree with you that their beliefs about gay relationships might be challenged.

Nan: You are saying that you didn't work with the social level, like the stereotypes they have about gay men, but you focused on their dreaming of what a gay man is.

Dawn: Yes, at that moment I am working with their dreaming process around what a gay man is. But our dreaming is often connected to our stereotypes that we have of people. One way to inadvertently work with stereotypes is to unfold the dreaming process connected to them. Then people learn that the qualities they see in others are parts of themselves and this loosens the stereotype from its object.

Ralph: Yes, what Nan is saying is that once they have that experience their stereotype changes.

Ursula: It is about the process in the background. Can you say more about the processes in the background?

Dawn: For this couple an unknown process in the background was a strong, firm and assertive energy, something that fought through lethargy and didn't give up. It was active and engaged. This is what they were looking for and what needed support. At that point I wasn't interested in whether he was gay or not. They were interested in staying together and this is important to me. However, there is no one way to explore ourselves sexually. Much sensitivity is needed in navigating the worlds of personal experience and the outer structures of our relationships.

Karen: In exploring sexuality, your experience must unfold to a certain level to make a conscious choice, to say I am this or I am that. He is in a committed relationship. He is having fantasies, but whether they are actually shifts in sexual identity comes much later.

Dawn: That is fascinating. What is sexual identity? Maybe if he wasn't in love with that particular woman, that particular soul or spirit, maybe he would now also open his heart to a man. I don't know if this makes him gay. It means he loved his wife and now loves a man.

Iris: I would like to bring up another point. Many people have said to me, "You are just fixed in your sexuality, and if you were really free you would be able to do it with anyone."

Ann: Is there an assumption that everybody, if they were whole, would be open to having sexual relationships with anybody no matter what their gender?

Dawn: This is a big question and I don't have any definitive answers. I think that everyone does have access to all possible experience. What moves each of us to live certain experiences is a mystery to me.

Ann: That seems like saying that if I am not open to everybody then I am not fluid, and that is a really hard position for me to be in and feel judged about.

Dawn: Absolutely. I hear that position. We can only follow our dreams and the unknown and irrational experience that is always trying to expand us. That is my point. Whatever your dreaming is telling you, whatever direction your impulses are pushing you towards is the right direction for you to be going. I don't think anyone can make a judgment about the spirit that guides our relationship and love life. That is my personal viewpoint. Do you want to say something more about that?

Ann: It is painful to feel a judgment from others that I am not being fluid because I am not open to a sexual relationship with a man. I am being psychologized. This is the underlying assumption in what you are saying. It is subtle and it is hard to defend myself in that position because as soon as I start defending myself, I am told that it just proves I am not fluid.

Iris: In fact I can be just as femme and just as butch with a female partner as I was when I was with male partners. I know you are not saying this, but I feel there is a background assumption that we are all basically bisexual. Let's get down to it. Isn't that a common assumption that people have? I don't agree with that.

Dawn: I would not emphasize the identity. I think identity is more limiting, although I do see its political and social necessity. I would say we are all dreaming, following the flow of experience in any given moment. That would be my viewpoint.

Iris: I would go with that.

Dawn: We are dreaming. I might define myself one way now, and you might identify yourself one way at this time, but how can we talk about what we are going to feel 20, 30, or 50 years from now? Who knows where the mysterious spirit of life will be leading us? And where was our dreaming leading us when we were ten or seventeen—do we then disavow past experiences by creating a set identity in the present?

Iris: Yes, I can be relatively solid in what I prefer to do. I can dream anything, but my freedom can go beyond gender, which means to me I don't have to play anymore with the other gender. You know what I mean? I can dream about meat and I am a vegetarian, and I can eat vegetables in a totally meaty way! (lots of laughter)

Nan: I find myself stuck in an idea. It is hard to remain fluid in thinking. I sometimes look at heterosexuals who have only had relationships with the opposite gender and feel judgmental. I think, "God, haven't you ever been attracted to someone of your gender?" It is just as hurtful for me to think that way and this is raising my consciousness about that.

Dawn: It was the one thing I was afraid to talk about and I am happy I did anyway, because I knew it would bring up so much diversity of opinion and I didn't want to hurt anyone.

Robin: Yeah, because we all struggle with it on different sides.

Dawn: The background pathology which is the basic seed of homophobia is what is so troublesome and painful and needs to be defended against.

Ann: It is also the conflict of being in a culture with whatever sexual identity you choose and the box that the culture puts you in. Even though your own sexual experience may have very little to do with who you are culturally. The box gets tighter.

Barb: I like the example you brought of the couple where the man was fascinated with being with a man. I think in couples, when one person has a fantasy of having an affair with somebody, they can also work it out in the same way. Like you said, how do you explain somebody who all of a sudden after 15 years goes out with a man? I want to throw in my viewpoint. Everybody has potential to have sex with either gender but I also really believe that people have their preference.

Ralph: You are saying that there is a valid reality; we have bodies and people identify as hetero, gay, lesbian, bisexual. But then you are adding that there is dreaming, and this is also a valid reality.

Dawn: Yes, and sometimes the dreaming emphasizes your preferences and furthers your development in that area, and other times your dreaming takes you other places.

Charles: For me there is so much richness in the other places. They get lost when I have to start to box it in right away. "Does this mean I am this or that?" Then we are not open to what happens. Years ago I was working in a training program with this man and I had an impulse to kiss him and I totally freaked out. "Oh, this means I am gay!" I had to work on that for a long time. I finally told the man how I felt. It turned into a whole process about love. At the end of the program I was kissing everybody. I was shy about being such a loving person, and this experience came out first with a man. All that richness gets lost by putting a label on it, doing it internally in a homophobic way, saying that my impulse means I am gay, so I don't dare trust.

Dawn: It stops your experience.

Charles: Yeah, it stops my experience and who knows what is there, what is going to come through. So that richness comes from being fluid and open.

Group Ghosts

This thought provoking discussion could have been the beginning of a group process. If we had had more time in this short lecture, it would have been rich to explore the polarization in our discussion more completely. A ghost is present. A hidden figure is being addressed, but it does not step forward and represent itself directly; this hidden figure disturbs communication and lies at the crux of our polarization. Ghost roles emerge in all group interactions. The ghost role is a part of group life that is disavowed, referred to as a position outside the group. It is a part of the group that might be spoken to or about, but not fully represented or identified with. In this case, the ghost can be characterized as the pathology police, the one who has ideas about what is healthy, moral, or most psychologically developed. It is a role or position that people feel and interact with, although it is not a role that stands directly for itself. Therefore, it acts as a ghost, a position in the group field that is difficult to pin down and wields great powers in its invisibility. This ghost is a frequent visitor in discussions and meetings within gay communities, and it is understandably one that would not be invited. However, to work more deeply with the group process would mean to name this ghost, and then to try to represent it and encourage interaction with it. Through interaction and inviting various viewpoints to come forward the group learns more about itself.[9]

In this discussion, the ghost can be noted in the group's references to other people's judgments and perceptions in addition to the internalized reality of these outer voices. In my efforts to speak about the fluid and mysterious nature of sexuality, I too was perceived as this ghost. In my bias I was caught valuing the fluid movements of nature and therefore, subtly devaluing its more static moments.

An Exercise

Exploring the depth and richness of our own sexuality and diversity of experience is key to getting beyond the veneer of tolerance. In so doing, many of us lose the ability to identify ourselves one way or another. We are simply explorers letting experience create us anew. This doesn't mean, as was stated in the previous group discussion, that one does not have preferences or that one cannot be in a monogamous relationship and discover sexual diversity while remaining in that relationship. Our fantasy and dreaming ability help us to learn more about ourselves and enrich the relationships that we have.

For these purposes of exploration I introduced an exercise in the lecture, that might also be of interest to the reader. In all due respect to the various sexual identities out there, this exercise does not indicate sexual identity or preference.

Make yourself comfortable, read each step of the exercise, and take time to experience it.

1. See if your mind will allow you to imagine each of the following:
   a) Can you imagine being a man and making love with a man?
   b) Can you imagine being a woman and making love with a woman?
   c) Can you imagine being a man and making love with a woman?
   d) Can you imagine being a woman and making love with a man?
2. Choose one of these four imaginary scenes that excites you, intrigues you, scares you or that you feel is most unknown and mysterious.
3. See if your mind will allow you to see that sexual scenario in great depth. Watch it unfold like a movie. Try and see yourself in that particular situation. See your body, your partner's body. Do you see a particular position that you are in? What are you feeling? Is there a part of yourself or your partner that you feel drawn to?
4. Try and notice in your fantasy something that attracts you, that seems maybe foreign or unusual, something that stands out to you or that you keep going back to in your mind, something that seems different from how you usually are sexually. It might be a position you are in. It could be having anatomy that you don't have. Is it a feeling, a tactile experience, a movement or sound that grabs your attention? Is it the way you look or a state that you get into that attracts you?
5. Keep your focus on this fascinating and unusual aspect without judging it. See if you can keep an open mind to explore it more deeply by amplifying and unfolding your experience. Amplify your experience by seeing, hearing, feeling or moving more intensely than you already are. Explore yourself in this new situation and try to discover the experience that is wanting to be had.
6. Reflect and ask yourself:
   a) Is your experience different from how you normally experience yourself—sexually or otherwise? Are there times when you do experience yourself this way? If so, when? Or do you fantasize about this aspect of yourself?
   b) Is that experience or state of mind something that you might bring into your intimate relationships?
   c) Does the state you experienced have something to do with a projection that you might have or have had on a group of people?

Examples

This exercise was a lot of fun and quite surprising for many of the people who attended this lecture. Here are some of the experiences and learnings that emerged.

One woman focused on her imagination of being a man making love with a woman. As the man she experienced a certain independence and initiative that captivated her. She was excited to discover this power in herself and to bring it into her relationships.

Another woman was drawn to the image of two men together. What struck her as she followed her fantasy was how unrelated the men were to one another in pursuing their own pleasure. "They just went after what they wanted and focused on getting their own needs met. They weren't pleasing, but just did what made them feel good regardless of their partner." After reflecting on her fantasy she realized she was often too pleasing and too adapted in her relationships, and needed to pursue her own needs and pleasure more, in and out of bed.

A man was afraid to unfold his fantasy of two men making love but courageously chose to zoom in on it. What scared him most was seeing one man penetrate the other. The one who was being penetrated seemed to create the most anxiety for him, so from the distance of the observer he imagined what it would be like. He then had an incredible experience of getting in touch with a certain receptivity that seemed very foreign and new for him.

One woman was surprised to discover that the negative projection she had onto a particular group of people transformed as she explored it internally. She claimed that she found something positive in a behavior that she had previously rejected.

Working with Homophobia

Discovering ourselves sexually can be exciting, and it can be frightening as well because it challenges our ideas about who we are. Exercises like the above are helpful in working with people who are homophobic, fearful or disgusted by homosexuality. A couple of years ago I worked with a man from Russia who noticed that he was very upset being in the United States and seeing all the gay men. He was not affected this way by lesbian women, he said, but found himself hateful of and disgusted by men.

We worked on it, and I asked him what was the most disgusting thing in his mind about two gay men. He said it was two men having sex.

I asked him to make a picture of the sexual scene that disturbed him the most. He said he saw two men fucking on all fours like dogs. In order to discover his experience of this scene, I used our hands to reenact it. I asked him to show me how that fucking went by pretending that my hand was one man and his was the other. He immediately rammed his hand into my hand as he imagined the two men engaging. We amplified his experience by focusing on his strong motion. Grinning from ear to ear he announced that he loved being so forceful. Soon a story emerged about how powerless he usually feels and how fearful he is to be overtly powerful and insistent due to his years living under Russian communism. He explained that his strength could never come out so directly because it would have been dangerous for him. Anything he wanted or stood for had to come out on the sly.

This man projected his overt force onto gay men and had developed a homophobic reaction that had little to do with sexuality but a lot to do with his own personal development. It is interesting to note that many gay men also feel they cannot be too overt with their full selves without risking their safety. On the other hand, many gay men stand proud in asserting their love.

In another situation a married woman was attracted to her best female friend and feared she was a lesbian. She was terrified, loved her husband, but couldn't get her mind off of her friend. Whenever they were together or she thought of her, she found herself very excited and turned on. She came from a fundamentalist Christian background and her feelings violently conflicted with those values. Not only was she fearful of these new feelings but she had internalized the negative beliefs instilled by her background.

She had been married for ten years and had two children. She felt she didn't have much in common with her husband and that sexuality was a central problem for them. He was interested in sex and she wasn't. I initially worked with her on her relationship with her husband, discovering what turned her off and supporting her to interact with him around these things. We also explored her feelings and fantasies about sleeping with her female friend. She imagined the experience to be very tender; she would be touched just right, there would be a lot of deep feeling and sensitivity. Since she wanted to keep her marriage, I encouraged her to bring this sensitivity into the relationship with her husband, to model it with him and to show him how to be more sensitive and feeling with her. I also encouraged her to show this same tenderness towards herself as she was making big changes. She should have patience, love and understanding for herself as well.

Over time she tried to make these changes with her husband, but the changes didn't satisfy her, and the feelings for her friend intensified. My approach was to be very patient and sensitive with her, modeling the behavior and experience she was searching for in her desire for her female friend.

This was long-term work, patiently and sensitively exploring all the fear and guilt around her fundamentalist background in addition to the tenderness and excitement that she felt toward women. Staying close to momentary experiences without pushing her, I encouraged her to just feel all of the differing experiences she was having. After a long while she decided she wanted to talk to her friend about her feelings and they slowly began a relationship.

Celebrating Gay Relationships

An essay about living and loving outside of the mainstream would not be complete without celebrating the special gifts and advantages of same sex relationships. Besides not needing birth control, there are various experiences to be proud of.

Those of us who are part of the sexual minority community provide a role model for how to live outside of mainstream relationship norms. This is not to negate those in heterosexual relationships, as many individuals radically challenge basic cultural relationship assumptions. However, those of us who live outside the mainstream have a pattern to stand for change, fluidity, and growth. We are pressed to take risks and stand for essential ideals that the mainstream might take for granted. This predicament offers a chance to develop a special strength and character.

Since gay relationships are excluded from the mainstream relationship culture, we are not expected to uphold certain mainstream relationship norms. This gives us a lot of freedom. The gift of exclusion is in not having to adapt; we don't just flow into the behaviors and relationship styles that popular culture and our families have reinforced—everything is wide open.

One example is that of gender roles. Mainstream culture has taught all of us particular behaviors and roles that govern the relationships between women and men. These gender roles are reinforced everywhere. Even though the women's and men's movements have been influential in opening people up to a variety of behaviors, there are still conventional gender roles that are very much a part of our culture. For example, my neighbors are curious to discover who in my relationship does the cooking and who mows the lawn.

In a same sex relationship, gender roles that we might have relied on as second nature come into question. Suddenly there is a big blank, an opening, a freedom! I remember my own earliest experiences sleeping with a woman; initiating sex or initiating relationship was a tremendous freedom. I didn't have to wait to be asked, to be approached, or await someone else's interest. I also didn't have to feel guilty about my own assertive nature, to think that I was doing something wrong or to worry that the man I was interested in would be turned off by my forwardness. This was a tremendous liberation to live and celebrate my natural expression of love and pursue my own desires. Of course, this is not limited to gay relationships; many women and men in all sorts of relationships are able to free themselves from these cultural roles. However, in a gay relationship, there is less struggle because there is no norm. A feeling of openness and discovery prevails as individuals gravitate to certain behaviors due to their nature rather than to a cultural expectation.

Another example is marriage. Many heterosexual couples fall into marriage as an expectation from culture. Since a gay couple is excluded from this institution, other options and relationship styles might open up.[10] Relationship is then structured by the spirit between the couple and not by an external formality. Relationship rituals emerge and are created from the relationship itself, not by cultural expectations or family pressures. Marriage for many might be more of a collective pressure than an authentic calling. Gay people are in the unique position of introducing different forms of relationships that are structured by the feelings and spirit of the relationship. All relationships needn't be tied in marriage; this does not mean that the relationship isn't valuable. This is not to say that straight people do not have these options; however, the temptation to follow existing norms is greater, whereas gay couples are forbidden to. Exclusion gives us a different perspective; it allows us to step back and evaluate what culture offers and then determine if it is a direction we would like to follow.

Another enormous gift that might or could come from living outside of mainstream relationship culture is spiritual rank. In his studies of group process, Arny Mindell noticed that different kinds of powers emerged in group life and were crucial for working on diversity and power issues.[11] Some individuals have a lot of social rank, meaning power that is given to them based on their status in society. Social rank includes skin color, gender, religion, age, and sexual orientation. Spiritual rank is an inner power that gives us the feeling of deep connection. It is a sense of well-being not contingent on external forces. A person with spiritual rank has gone through a lot in life and has been able to maintain some center or balance in spite of great injustice. Through life's turbulence and injustice, such a person goes down to the bottom and then discovers a spiritual center. This inner feeling gives an individual a great inner power, a deep confidence and self-love that comes from the depths of their being. This is a treasure that many people who have been marginalized uncover when the outer world has shut them out.

The Central Challenge

There are many external difficulties that confront those of us who live and love outside of the mainstream. For most of us not a day goes by where something in the world is not offensive or exclusive. However, the most crucial challenge happens inwardly.

One of the most dangerous side effects of living outside of the mainstream relationship culture is feeling outside internally. It is one thing to feel rejected outwardly, but more painful and insidious is to feel outside inside of ourselves. Hardly perceptible, the daily residue of cultural exclusion and moral judgment lodges itself to soft and vulnerable tissue, hurting the heart and brainwashing the mind until we are cringing from ourselves and excluding our own humanity. The subtle feeling attitudes of insecurity and inferiority that many of us have are the greatest casualty. These feelings are not often spoken about publicly because there is a need to show a strong front. It is a war zone, and when people are at war they protect themselves and don't show their wounds and agony. However, many wars might resolve more quickly if we did. I remember a few years ago when the Process Work Center of Portland held a town meeting to address the difficulties and conflict that arose from Ballot Measure 9, the first anti-gay rights initiative introduced by the Oregon Citizen's Alliance (OCA), a right wing fundamentalist Christian group.[12] After the meeting, one of the leading OCA officials reported that he had been unaware that the gay community was suffering so much. Apparently, he previously had not seen the personal pain and hardship that many of the gay participants expressed.

Much of the suffering is not visible, particularly the inner attitudes and psychological hardship that we undergo. Some of the behavior is so subtle that it might seem insignificant, but it has a profound impact on self-esteem. It is behavior that is automatic: it is the way we accommodate the straight world by treating ourselves as second class citizens in order to make the mainstream feel more comfortable. It is the way we sneak around and try to not upset people with our affection; it comes out in the way we sometimes assert our strength and look arrogant when we feel hurt. It is perceptible when our heart rate goes up when we have to tell the hotel clerk that we do really want a double bed. It can be noticed sitting next to a friendly person on an airplane who has asked us about our work, and we begin to perspire because we know the next question will be if we are married. It is in our subtle and unspoken self-hatred, the way we feel when we don't fit in, the way we are treated and feel in family gatherings, particularly relative to straight siblings and spouses. Finally we can notice it in the constant fear and turmoil of whether to speak up or stay silent in the numerous situations that emerge in just one day.

The most overt expression of grappling with the internalized effects of collective hatred is suicide. It is no coincidence that gay identified or gay curious youth are at the highest risk of suicide amongst young people in the United States.[13]

I am no longer certain that internalized homophobia can be overcome. Managed, worked with, and dealt with from moment to moment, yes. Eradicated? I don't think so. In fact, I no longer see it as a personal issue to be worked on solely in the confines of therapy or other personal work. Personal growth, self-knowledge and therapy are all important, but I do not think we can develop in isolation from the external culture we are living in. Individuals cannot feel well until the culture as a whole develops. My internalized homophobia is just as much everyone's problem as it is mine, just as internalized racism is not simply a painful issue for people of color, but a painful and humiliating problem for us all.

As long as the world splits off its own sexuality, psychological, political and social oppression are imminent. The process of splitting is what creates "pathology." When we split off experience, we see it as other, as outside of ourselves—as sick, not us. The inner feeling of being sick or not normal is one of the worst kinds of oppression. This is why when people say they are tolerant, I feel disgusted. Tolerance is not what I am looking for. Tolerance tells me that you stand above me and allow me to exist. You are in the position to allow, to accept or reject, to tolerate or not to—you have the power. Tolerance says that you are not a part of me, that we are separate and that you have more power. I will accept nothing less than celebration in my life. If I accept less, I feel downed, I feel less. I have given you the power inside of me and outside of me to separate yourself from me. I won't let you do it. I have inadvertently encouraged the split, the pathology, both internally and externally. If you see me accepting your tolerance, you see me accepting myself as a second class citizen. You are seeing that I feel so hurt and downed and desperate that I will take any crumb you offer me, and as a result I have accepted myself as less than you. Therefore, I am much more interested in encouraging and challenging the mainstream to develop itself; tolerance is cheap and safe. It does nothing to challenge the deeper structure around sexuality and create genuine sustainable change.

End Notes

[1] Adapted from a lecture given by the author at the Process Work Center of Portland, in Portland, Oregon, May 9, 1996.
[2] From the CD, *Blacks' Magic,* New York, London Records, 1990.
[3] Arnold Mindell, *The Dreambody in Relationships* (London: Routledge and Kegan Paul, 1987).
[4] Arnold Mindell, *The Dreambody in Relationships* and *Working with the Dreaming Body.*
[5] For more information about unintentional signals, see Working with the Dreaming Body, and Joseph Goodbread, *The Dreambody Toolkit* (London: Routledge and Kegan Paul, 1987) and *Radical Intercourse: How Dreams Unite Us In Love, Conflict and Other Inevitable Relationships* (Portland OR: Lao Tse Press, 1997).
[6] See Goodbread's *Radical Intercourse* for an in-depth exploration of dreaming up. Chapter 12 particularly focuses on the dreaming up phenomenon in regard to group fields and social issues.
[7] See letters to the editor in *Just Out,* published in Portland, Oregon, particularly issues from February through April 1997.
[8] *Just Out,* Portland, Oregon, Volume 14, Number 12, from the editorial: 3. Quoted from Karen Shoffner, Front Page, North Carolina.
[9] See Mindell's *Sitting in the Fire,* for information on ghost roles and group process work.
[10] As this work comes to press, there has been much national controversy about gay marriage. President Clinton signed the infamous Defense of Marriage Act (DOMA) which defines marriage as the union between a man and a woman. Numerous states have recently implemented legislation that would inhibit gay marriage and bar recognition of gay unions from other states. Hawaii almost became the first state to legalize gay marriage, but lost that battle. In 2000, Vermont legalized civil unions giving gay couples most of the state's rights that heterosexual couples enjoy.
[11] Arnold Mindell, *Sitting in the Fire.*
[12] This meeting was held at Portland State University, on October 4, 1993. Approximately 250 people attended this meeting, which was then broadcast on cable television. This broadcast is regularly repeated.

[13] A study compiled by the Hetrick Martin Institute in New York in 1992 revealed that gay teenagers are two to three times more likely to commit suicide than heterosexual teens. The Secretaries Task Force on Youth Suicide at the Department of Human Services in 1989 also reported similar findings.

The Abnormal Beliefs Initiative

In 1992 Oregon became the first state to introduce the "Abnormal Behaviors" initiative, a ballot measure designed to severely limit the civil rights of homosexuals, and to equate same sex relationships with pedophilia and bestiality. Nationwide, all eyes were on Oregon as it anxiously awaited the outcome of this first anti-gay rights initiative, which later inspired similar measures throughout the United States. When the measure was defeated by a slight margin, many of us breathed a sigh of relief, only to find a similar but less strongly worded measure on the ballot in 1994.

I spent election night glued to the television screen watching the close race unfold. At midnight newscasters were predicting a narrow defeat for Measure 13. Emotionally exhausted, I went to bed and fell into a deep sleep. I woke up the following morning giddy with amusement. The strangest fantasy had come to me in the night; it offered humor and a little detachment from the knowledge that nearly half the population of Oregon had voted to sanction discrimination against gay people.

My fantasy begins in the front of any-mall-USA where I am gathering signatures for a proposed initiative to amend the Oregon Constitution. The "Abnormal Beliefs" initiative reads as follows:

Text of Proposed Initiative to Amend the Oregon Constitution

This state shall not recognize any categorical provision for heterosexual, Christian fundamentalists. This includes similar categories such as pedophiles, white supremacy groups (i.e., the Ku Klux Klan, Neo-Nazis), and right wing militia groups. Quotas, affirmative action or any special status shall not apply to those who hold these beliefs or exhibit these forms of conduct, nor shall the government promote these behaviors or beliefs.

State, regional, local governments and their properties and monies shall not be used to promote, encourage, or facilitate the beliefs of heterosexual, fundamentalist Christians, pedophiles, white supremacists and right wing militia groups.

State, regional and local governments and their departments, agencies and other entities, including specifically the State Department of Higher Education and the public schools, shall assist in setting a standard for Oregon's youth that recognizes the beliefs of heterosexual, fundamentalist Christians, pedophiles, white supremacists and right wing militia groups as abnormal, wrong, unnatural and perverse, and that these behaviors and beliefs are to be discouraged and avoided.

Arguments in Favor

My fantasy continues as I visualize the voter information pamphlet and the arguments in favor of the initiative that I would submit for publication.

Introduction. White, heterosexual, Christian fundamentalists have become too powerful politically and we must stop them now. Their agenda has infiltrated the moral, social and political fabric of this country. As an organized, powerful lobbying group, they are on the verge of totally dominating the Republican party. They also have dangerous ties to white supremacist and right wing militia groups.

On Political Power and Special Rights. Individuals will have just as much opportunity to choose to indulge in heterosexual, fundamentalist Christian behavior as before. This initiative will, however, prevent them from obtaining special rights and it will prevent the government from using our taxes to support their beliefs and values. For too long, white, heterosexual, fundamentalist Christians have enjoyed the privilege of a tacit affirmative action which has made them a dominant presence in the work force of this country to the exclusion of others. These implicit quotas have existed over the centuries since the dominance of the Christian Church. This initiative will finally put a stop to the special rights of white, heterosexual Christian fundamentalists.

On Public Education. We believe that the average Oregonian is unaware of the many disturbing aspects of the heterosexual Christian fundamentalist movement, including the fact that these values are currently being advocated in our public schools and funded by our taxes. Curriculums based on European, heterosexual, Christian fundamentalist beliefs promote an absolute view of the world, and thereby discourage the diversity of human experience, whether it be expressed in thought, religion, communication style, dress code, human relationships, ethnicity, or the arts. In this wonderful and diverse world of ours, one-sided absolute beliefs teach our children to fear what they do not know and limit their own capacity to think freely. These values lead to supremacist beliefs and the fear of others, which have increased the amount of bias and hate-related crime and violence.

On Sexuality. Without the freedom and openness to address human sexuality in our schools we are in danger of putting our children at risk for sexually transmitted diseases and unwanted pregnancies. Sexual ignorance spreads misinformation and conceals important information that might be essential for our youth. Furthermore, it should be noted that gay teens are at the highest risk for suicide amongst all youth and that the prevailing educational and cultural atmosphere around homosexuality has a direct correlation to this statistic. Heterosexual Christian fundamentalist values that have controlled the curriculum in our schools are directly responsible for the growing numbers of sexually transmitted diseases, unwanted pregnancies and suicide; we must save our children from such destructive beliefs.

On Sexual Abuse. Studies show a disproportionate percentage of sexual abuse and incest amongst families with rigid sexual values. It has long been established that rigidly regulating sexuality does not inhibit sexual behavior but creates an environment of secrecy where these behaviors are concealed and are then often expressed abusively, particularly with children who are too weak to defend themselves. The imposition of rigid sexual values from the heterosexual, fundamentalist Christian coalition has a direct result on these rising occurrences of sexual abuse.

Heterosexual fundamentalist Christians prey on our children, recruiting them into their lifestyle in an attempt to become a more powerful social and political force.

In Summary. These individuals can be helped. This initiative is meant to condemn and curtail the beliefs and behaviors of heterosexual, fundamentalist Christians, but is in no way an attack on their individual persons. Studies show that such individuals have come from abusive backgrounds with dominating fathers and passive mothers. Violence, emotional deprivation and strong authority enforce their beliefs with little input allowed from other sources. Stepping out of this pathological childhood background is almost impossible due to the intense fear of disobeying authority. These people then become the dominating authorities they feared as children and insist on their absolute beliefs for others.

The only reason for filing this initiative is because the heterosexual Christian fundamentalist movement is close to achieving its political goals. Let's say no to special rights and stop the dominance of fundamentalist beliefs in our schools, government and social agencies.

On the Way to Victory

My fantasy unfolds further: I am thrilled! Over the past nine months my team and I have managed to gather the necessary 90,000 signatures of registered Oregon voters to put the proposed initiative on the ballot. We distributed the arguments in favor wherever we went. Some people tore them up right on the spot. Others laughed and supported us from a distance. Fortunately, there were enough concerned citizens who were convinced by our cause and saw the seriousness of this issue.

There is a lot of controversy and many claim that the initiative is unconstitutional. However, I am encouraged by the strong citizen support and letters I get from like-minded individuals who have had enough of the cultural, political and social domination by heterosexual, Christian fundamentalists.

Fame

Never before has anyone dared to introduce an initiative such as this. Not only are local newspapers and television networks eager to interview me, but I am wanted by the national and international media as well. Oprah asked me to appear on her show. At this point I have turned down all offers, even though I love Oprah. I have also received my share of negative publicity, including quite a bit of hate mail. I now have an unlisted phone number and rarely pick up my telephone. Various churches have been trying to contact me and the religious community is particularly up in arms. Oregon newspapers are filled with controversial editorials. However, despite the negative and hostile climate, I do believe we are doing the right thing.

Although I have been hounded by the media, I am strategically waiting to hold my first public press conference. I am silently enjoying the dialogue and debate. My plan is to speak one month before election day.

The Press Conference

I can't believe I have been able to keep silent for so long! Today is the big day. I called the press conference a couple of days ago and was informed the next day that it had to be moved to a larger venue because the national media would also be there. My statements were to be broadcast throughout the country on the evening news. I guess my silence created much mystique.

I am nervous and excited as I stand behind a podium with more microphones than I have ever seen in my life. This is my big moment. I inform the group that I have only one statement to make. I begin speaking:

> To the citizens of Oregon, the people of the United States and those listening from abroad:
>
> Please **DO NOT** vote for the Abnormal Beliefs Initiative. Any initiative that excludes and/or isolates any group of people is dangerous to us all. No majority should ever have the legal means or access to legitimize discrimination or to legally dominate with their values. In the United States we are still weeding out the remnants of unchecked legalized oppression and discrimination. Ours is a history that includes domination and tyranny; it is a history that we all suffer from and it is present today. Vote against me and people like me, and like you, who every day in some way exclude or isolate or dominate others. We all have this tendency, so let's be aware of it and learn together about getting along with difference.
>
> Thank you for listening to me. I plead and encourage you all to vote against this initiative and send a resounding message throughout the world against discrimination, tyranny and social control.

From the moment I began to speak, I watched as hundreds of jaws went slack and eyes narrowed, trying to make sense of what had just been said. Heads shook in disbelief and tilted forward to hear again what they had thought was a slip of the tongue. When no reassurance came, some sat back, and I could see small smiles form over the first stages of shock.

Crossing the Great Divide: A Look at Gender

Looking Gay

I was recently in a psychology training seminar with a diverse group of people, including many of my friends and colleagues. We had just watched a young man do some personal work and were involved in a learning discussion. Suddenly, someone said, "He looked gay to me." Others chimed in, "Yeah, wasn't he?" I noticed my shoulders tense and my spine tighten. I couldn't believe what I was hearing! This man had mentioned he had a girlfriend. He spoke about his past and related a very heterosexual history. "What does a gay person look like?" I blurted out.

I went home that evening rather disturbed. How could I be so fired up and see things so differently from friends and colleagues I respect and love dearly? My agitation stimulated my reflection. I wouldn't feel at ease until I got to the bottom of this.

Is being gay an ethnicity? Can one look gay as one might look Italian, Mexican, or Scandinavian? As far as I knew, homosexuality went beyond ethnic borders. Was it a common culture that people were seeing? The young man who bared his soul at the seminar was not part of any gay culture I was aware of. Was it in his clothing or hairstyle? He wore jeans and a T-shirt, and nothing stood out to me about his hairstyle. Is there such thing as a gay hairstyle or gay clothing? Are there stores that only sell gay clothes that I haven't yet been alerted to?

In all due respect, my head hasn't been entirely in the sand; I am aware that the gay community has created and embraced various fashion trends throughout history. Much of this "gay look" has been due to the need for an identity, and for a common signal to notice one another in a culture that makes us invisible. However, at a time when gay visibility and gay issues are more prevalent than ever before, there is a much greater diversity of gay people. (Actually, there always has been.) No, this is something deeper than clothing.

Portland, Oregon's former police chief, Tom Potter, the proud father of a gay daughter who is a police officer in the city of Portland, said that he knew his daughter was gay because she liked to wear jeans and didn't like wearing dresses.[1] A man tells me that he always knew he was gay because he liked to dress up in his mother's clothes. Or how about this snippet of dialogue between mother and daughter from April Sinclair's coming of age novel, *Ain't Gonna Be the Same Fool Twice:*

"You're not one of them. And I know for a fact that you weren't born gay."

"How do you know that?"

"Because I carried you for nine months, that's how. I knew you before you knew yourself. There has never been anything abnormal about you. You weren't even a decent tomboy. If you had some boy in you, I would've picked it up a long time ago."[2]

The character of Mama Stevenson, steeped in ignorance and fear, directly names one of the most prevalent and hurtful stereotypes that gay people encounter—gender. From her perspective, being gay means you have crossed the gender divide, that God gave you too much of the opposite gender. Mama says it outright. Others are more subtle, and allude to crossing gender borders by referring to clothing or activities that have been seen as gender specific, such as sports and mechanics or hairstyling and ballet.

Beyond the stereotypes and the cutting judgment is a clue, one possible answer to my query. "Looking gay" means you have broken out of gender roles. This transgression might be manifest in clothing and hairstyle, gestures and mannerisms, or activities and interests. But why is the rejection of gender roles analogous to homosexuality? How did the two become equated with one another?

Gender Roles in Relationships

It is no coincidence that in our schools the biggest playground insult is to call your schoolmate a sissy, faggot, homo, lesbo, or dyke. Usually these insults are prompted by behavior that does not go along with gender expectations. The sensitive boy who cares little for sports and likes to spend time quietly drawing and dreaming will begin lifting weights so the kids don't call him a fag. His father might try to "toughen him up" by demanding he do physical activity and taunt him by challenging his male identity. When a boy displays attributes that are not culturally sanctioned for his gender, his environment quickly fears he might be gay. Who knows if he has even had a sexual fantasy or attraction at this point in his life! Nevertheless, the culture has taken a strong step in fearing and shaping the sexual behavior of this boy based on its interpretation of gender, not his natural predisposition.

From this perspective, gender roles appear to be a cultural construction. Gender specific behaviors, mannerisms and activities are assigned, created, and supported by culture. But when we are free to follow our inner natures, personal inclinations, and abilities, gender roles begin to break down. The individual who feels compelled to develop her inner nature rather than adapt to societal structures might find herself on the other side of the gender barrier. How might her behavior then influence both heterosexual and homosexual relationships?

Since gender roles mold us by repressing and supporting different aspects of ourselves, gender roles in relationships are highly influential. From a young age most of us have witnessed the roles in heterosexual relationships in a variety of circumstances. We have unconsciously made note of the gender roles and know the ones with which we are supposed to identify. Even in our modern world, there is little diversity in the mainstream images we see of heterosexual couples and the gender behaviors that they display. As far as gay relationships go, the mainstream hardly sees them.

If the mainstream structure of heterosexual relationship seems primarily governed by gender roles, the woman or man who has developed outside of these parameters will feel limited in such a relationship. From this perspective, gay relationship might be more inviting. Without the constraint of gender roles, the individual is free to explore herself in a variety of ways.

I remember my first experience in a gay relationship, the surprise and freedom that came from the lack of gender roles. As two women, our individual natures, not our gender, determined our behavior with one another and the roles that we occupied in the relationship. The expectation to fulfill a certain role was absent. I particularly recall feeling free to pursue and initiate interaction and sexual intimacy, something I had slightly repressed or felt guilty about in my relationships with men.

I must be careful here not to imply that this sense of freedom in same sex relationships is a cause for homosexuality. First, I am not interested in the cause for homosexuality (or heterosexuality), because seeking a cause implies that there is something wrong with homoerotic love. Second, sexuality is awesomely complex and I have no idea what deeper spirit draws all sorts of people together. Last, this discussion about gender explores the dynamic area where gender and sexuality overlap. Obviously, there are gay people whose nature mirrors more conventional gender roles and there are straight people who have totally shaken up the meaning of gender in their relationships. Gender presents us with different challenges in both gay and straight relationships and remains a rich garden for growth.

Any relationship that dictates a form of behavior that does not go along with our nature is a turn off. We lose interest in relationship when we are forced to leave out vital aspects of ourselves. Where gender roles rule, individual growth stops and relationships stagnate. Any relationship that offers a freedom to explore beyond gender is a turn on because it allows us to experience more of who we are.

Crossing Borders

In 1997, the *New York Times* ran a story about adolescent sexuality stemming from the public panic that broke out when several groups of girls attending private secondary schools announced that they were lesbian. The main point of the article was to calm parents' fear that their children might be gay, through stating that adolescence is a time of sexual experimentation. In an attempt to educate and reassure parents, Dr. Kenneth J. Zucker, head of the Child and Adolescent Gender Identity Clinic at the Clarke Institute of Psychiatry in Toronto, stated that childhood play preferences between the ages of two and four are the strongest predictors of sexual orientation. "The more extensive a child's pattern of cross-gender behavior during childhood, the more likely he or she will be gay." He goes on to say that this is not a definite determining factor and is less so for girls than for boys.[3]

Dr. Zucker's conclusions might have some significance. However, his data is tainted in that he is looking for a cause of homosexuality. He admits that his evidence is not conclusive and that desire is a more complex process; clearly, there are too many people in gay relationships who have embraced more conventional gender behaviors as children and adults. The significance of his observation lies in the definition of gender behavior that our culture embraces, and in his own bias which comes forth in upholding this viewpoint. The real study should be about gender and culture, not about homosexuality. From this perspective, one might hypothesize that heterosexual relationships can be limiting if we develop parts of ourselves beyond the gender divide.

One of the fascinating bits of data is that his theory is less true for girls than for boys. This is the key to a discovery which again has less to do with the cause of homosexuality and more to do with culture and gender roles. My guess is that his theory is less true for girls because our culture is loosening up and allowing girls more access to behavior that had previously been left in the domain of males. In 1972, before the advent of Title IX, which gave females equal opportunity in school and athletics, 7.5% of all athletes in American high schools were female. Now that figure is 40%.[4] In 1972, only one in 27 high school girls played sports: today that figure is one in three.[5] In other words, the rough and tumble activities that Dr. Zucker refers to as male preferences seem to be more determined by cultural acceptance and not inherent in any innate gender preference. However, we have not yet come as far in broadening our ideas of appropriate behavior when it comes to our male children. Boys who venture outside accepted gender behavior appear to meet with less collective support.

One of the conclusions I come to from Dr. Zucker's study is that many gay people are role models who shake up our consensus view of gender reality and challenge us to explore all of who we are. Our preoccupation with gender is an attempt to get to know ourselves better. Too often we take for granted what it means for us to be a woman or a man and rely on stereotypes and cultural definitions. But what, if anything, does it mean to each of us to be the gender we are? What is it like to have the kinds of bodies and physical experiences that we have? What has culture taught us about ourselves and what are the images and experiences that come from deep within us? These are highly individual experiences that often lose their vitality because they are presupposed by culture.

Gender and Cultural Edges

If we follow our dreams and focus on our personal development, most of us will find that gender roles are too limiting for all of who we are. We are constantly crossing, or being challenged to cross, the gender divide. Indeed, we have aspects to our personality with which we are more comfortable, and where we feel we know ourselves, and this familiar ground comprises our identity. On the other hand, our dream lives are populated with figures and energies that often do not go along with our closely coveted view of ourselves. The man who dreams of the seductive sexy woman awakens happily to have had contact with this figure in his dreams, but he might not realize that *he* is also this woman. A part of him is seductive and displays the kinds of characteristics that his dream figure does, and he needs more contact with them. The woman who dreams of a rough and tough man needs some of that energy in her life. One-sidedness in any sort of identity appears to be compensated by a universal drive towards wholeness.

Recently I worked with a powerful and successful businessman who was having trouble getting close to women. He had dreamed of a little girl playing in a field of flowers. When we began to explore the characteristics of this little girl in the flower field, he discovered a part of himself that was sensitive and shy, a beautiful and precious part of him! Yet it was very difficult for him to identify with this aspect, which could potentially assist him in his desire to be more intimate in his relationships. The difficulty for individuals in getting closer to their dream images is in part due to their association of those qualities with the opposite gender roles. This becomes an enormous threat to the identity.

Gender roles present us with some of our biggest edges to development. Edges are the composite beliefs and philosophies that keep our known world in place and make it difficult for us to grow into new parts of ourselves.[6] Individuals at the edge of crossing the gender divide will say, "I can't do that, only men do that," or "that is too feminine or masculine," or "my husband would leave me if I started to wear the pants," or "my friends would think I was a sissy," and so on. These typical fears and beliefs are voiced at the edges of our cultural identification with gender roles.

At the bottom of these comments lies the fear that we are not our gender; we are not real men or real women. Gender is one of our most basic identities; if it feels threatened, our entire being feels totally devastated. We feel like freaks of nature, like we don't belong. Who and what are we without gender? Consequently, when people develop parts of themselves that are outside the parameters of our cultural consensus constituting gender, they are crossing a major collective edge and find themselves having to defend their biological gender.

Women's sports have been plagued by the gender dilemma and the gay shadow that seems to follow it. In the exciting historical year of 1996–97, we saw the birth of two women's professional basketball leagues in the United States. This development has been a long time in coming and its promoters have been doing all they can to insure its success.[7] Apparently, part of this success means presenting a "feminine" image of the women who play the sport in order not to turn off the general public. At a promotional talk for our local team in Portland, the public relations woman made sure to inform us that the team looked just gorgeous modeling evening gowns in a fashion show for one of the local stores. I failed to see the relevance to basketball. Another player felt moved to tell us that she liked men, "really liked them," and gave us a knowing wink. I was sad and angry that the team felt they had to do such a promotion in order to survive. Upholding traditional images of gender roles is so important that professional women athletes are often assumed to be gay and must adamantly insist against this image.

Television has aired many wonderful commercials supporting women's sports, particularly basketball. But in some of the commercials and interviews with the players, I find it humiliating and jarring to hear these athletes say, "Women can play basketball and still be feminine." "We like to be aggressive on the court, but feel feminine and ladylike off the court." "We like playing ball but like to dress up and put on makeup and high heels." Who are they talking to? Why do they have to defend their gender? They have to defend themselves because they have crossed the gender divide; engaging in competitive sports is not perceived as innately female. How painful that they must insist that they are women, and in doing so uphold a conventional view of womanhood, instead of standing for the women they are. Rita Mae Brown's novel *Sudden Death*[8] describes the advent of women's professional tennis and the similar humiliations these women were put through in order to sell women's tennis to the general public. One would have hoped for some change in the last twenty-five years. However, for many, the cultural consequence of breaking out of gender roles still carries the collective burden of proving that one is truly a man or a woman, and also that one is heterosexual.

What Are Femininity and Masculinity?

I have never heard a male athlete say that he likes to be aggressive on the court but still feel masculine. Why is his masculinity equivalent to his athletic prowess, and femininity devoid of any athleticism? What are masculinity and femininity really?

At a relationship workshop I led, two women who didn't know each other very well volunteered to work on their relationship by demonstrating an exercise. Although Kristi and Joan had first met at the workshop, there was a good feeling between them. About five minutes into the exercise, Kristi looked at Joan and told her that she enjoyed her intelligence and her sharpness but sensed there was something feminine and soft that Joan wanted to learn more about. Joan's eyes froze, her smile lost its life as it remained pasted to her face, and her body literally deflated as she sank into the ground. Kristi noticed nothing and went on chattering while Joan's smile faded and her head fell into her hands. Joan was devastated, could barely express herself, and ended up in a puddle of tears.

The soft or tender quality that Kristi might have been searching for in Joan, and also unconsciously in herself, perhaps would be rich learning for both of them. However, equating those qualities with gender is hurtful. It gives Joan the feeling that she is less of a woman, that there is something innately wrong with her. Additionally, it demeans the intelligent and sharper aspects of Joan's personality and makes her feel ashamed instead of proud.

A man in my practice confides in me with great embarrassment and fear that he is here to work on his masculinity. His face is drooping and he looks like a beaten soul. He tells me that his wife has told him he isn't man enough. I tell him I don't know what that means, nor do I know what masculinity is. He looks at me, bewildered. I tell him that he looks like a great man to me and that masculinity is a word with little meaning or substance; it is more hurtful and limiting than helpful. His eyes widen, inviting a glimmer of hope. He explains to me that his wife accuses him of letting people walk all over him, of not demanding credit for his work, and that he generally finds it difficult to assert himself with people.

Working on his presenting problem, we discover that he is a sensitive and caring man, and also rather introverted. It turns out that he often holds himself back because he is sensitive to the needs of others. As a teenager he had vowed to himself that he would never be like his tyrannical father who selfishly put his needs before everyone else's. Paradoxically, his sensitivity is actually his greatest gift to self-assertion. When he identifies more completely with his sensitivity, he is able to stand for his deepest feelings. This emerged particularly in relationship to his wife. He proudly stood for how hurt he felt by her cutting comments about his manhood and demanded that she be more open and sensitive.

Developing "masculinity" and "femininity" have become buzz words for individuals focused on their personal growth. People say that they are working on the masculine or feminine sides of themselves, and they recommend it for others as well. However, I can't help but notice the pathologizing attitude that drives them as they strive for an ideal that limits rather than expands, and subtly wounds self-esteem. As a result, many people do not discover and appreciate the inherent beauties of their individual natures.

As a whole, psychology inadvertently reflects this pathologizing tendency by deeming some behaviors more appropriate and creating norms of health. A psychology that upholds a model of behavior falls into the dangerous practice of maintaining collective attitudes in order to keep the status quo. Just as disavowed aspects of individual psychology are fertile grounds for self-discovery and beckon us in our dreams, so do collective aspects of behavior that have been marginalized. Any psychology that *only* reinforces a collectively accepted identity misses opportunities for profound transformation. Psychology has had a mixed history in regard to gender issues; it has at times enforced certain collective norms that have enslaved women or men who deviated from them, and at other times has supported individual freedom and the impulse to break out of confining roles.

The trend in psychology that emphasizes balance in developing both the feminine and masculine can be commended in its attempt to further our wholeness. The critical point is in how we define this wholeness. If we separate aspects of ourselves into masculine and feminine, we create formidable cultural borders and begin to arbitrarily define what manhood and womanhood are. My view is that the definitions of man and woman are as diverse as the individual men and women who create them.

If, as a therapist, I exclusively accept my clients' viewpoint that they need to be more masculine or feminine, I am unconsciously siding with a collective belief that they identify with, and colluding against another part of them that is not confined to these definitions of behavior. I need to be aware that there are cultural beliefs around gender that may or may not go along with an individual's nature and that these beliefs could be inhibiting or hurting other parts of them. I also need to know that by assuming I understand what a client means when he or she uses the labels of masculine or feminine, I inadvertently side with a cultural definition of gender and miss the specific behavior my client refers to. This is why I always ask clients what these words mean and never assume that I know what they are talking about, because I don't. I find my attitude usually relieves people, who then feel free to explore themselves without the yoke of gender inadequacy weighing them down.

Interestingly, often the gender-defined behavior that the client wants to rid herself of or embrace is unconsciously present in the conflict itself.

For example, a woman says that she is too masculine and wants to develop her feminine side. I discover that her understanding of masculine is that she feels she is too rough and pushy. She wants to be more receptive. She is unaware of how her roughness is present in how she relentlessly pushes herself to be feminine, and that this attitude is what is hurting her. She is actually too receptive to her own well-meaning ideas about her development and is unaware how hurt she feels by them.

By assigning behavior to gender and labeling ourselves accordingly, we not only create limiting roles, but our experience of gender becomes static; we grow blind to its dynamic nature. Remember the man whose wife accused him of being unmanly and who wanted him to stand up for himself more? She had a specific idea of what being more manly meant, and he was partially in agreement with her viewpoint. However, he was unaware of how these set conventional ideas about masculinity prevented him from seeing the deeper aspects of his nature that he wanted to stand for. If masculinity becomes attached to stereotypical images, it loses its fresh and unmediated quality.

Categorizing behavior freezes our gifts by making them less accessible and keeps the gender divide firmly in place. Qualities that naturally reside in each of us dare not unfold for fear of collective condemnation. The gender gap widens as these same qualities are only perceived and welcomed in the other. Development becomes focused on the gender of the other and the quality itself loses its innate and individual expression. My approach to lifting this gender hypnosis is to appreciate individual experience anew in every situation and let it unfold and define itself.[9]

Gender and History

Gender definition is greatly influenced by the interaction of various cultures. Gender identity has differences and similarities depending on the culture and country you are from. Furthermore, our definition of gender evolves with our history and the times. For example, in white European-American culture, the frail, delicate and passive lady became equated with femininity in the 19th century, a direct result of the industrial revolution, which stripped women of the manufacturing work they had done in the home. Before the industrial revolution, products such as clothing, soaps, candles, and all practical necessities were made by women. Men worked the land, often with the help of women as well; domestic and physical work was shared and was mutually respected.

> When manufacturing moved out of the home and into the factory, the ideology of womanhood began to raise the wife and mother as ideals. As workers, women had at least enjoyed economic equality, but as wives, they were destined to become appendages to their men, servants to their husbands. As mothers, they would be defined as passive vehicles for the replenishment of human life.[10]

Angela Davis deepens this discussion by showing how the historical experience of African American women deviated considerably from the mainstream white gender norms. The history and legacy of slavery in the United States is one of the most horrendous and heinous crimes of our times. The inhuman view that saw all black people as beasts of burden did not adhere to the gender roles of the times. Gender roles had no meaning in slavery and the frail lady was not instilled in African consciousness. Davis points out that a side effect from such cruel and inconceivable oppression was that the playing field between black men and women was leveled. Furthermore, when survival is of the essence, everyone's natural qualities and abilities are needed and appreciated.

> Black women were equal to their men in the oppression they suffered; they were their men's social equals within the slave community; and they resisted slavery with a passion equal to their men's. This was one of the greatest ironies of the slave system, for in subjecting women to the most ruthless exploitation conceivable, exploitation which knew no sex distinctions, the groundwork was created not only for Black women to assert their equality through their social relations, but also to express it through their acts of resistance.[11]

Therefore, it is no surprise that in 1851 in Akron, Ohio, at an all-white convention discussing women's rights, it was a heroic black woman who challenged the gender divide and sent a resounding message in one of the most powerful speeches in American history. Sojourner Truth's "Ain't I a Woman" speech challenged white European sexism and gender roles and brilliantly reminded the audience of the brutal reality of slavery.

> I have ploughed and planted, and gathered into barns and no man could head me! And ain't I a woman? I could work as much and eat as much as a man—when I could get it—and bear the lash as well! And ain't I a woman? I have borne thirteen children and seen them

most all sold off to slavery, and when I cried out with my mother's grief, none but Jesus heard me! And ain't I a woman?[12]

With booming voice and muscular frame, Sojourner Truth defied the frail image of the female gender and challenged the collective definitions of gender.

The Hidden Gender Dilemma

What would you do if you gave birth to a baby with ambiguous genitalia? This "condition" is known as intersexuality or hermaphroditism. Approximately one in two thousand babies are born with genitalia that defy male/female gender categories.[13] In the United States, specialists determine whether the infant would be better suited to live as a male or female; surgery, in combination with hormone treatment, often life-long, is the most common solution. "Genital ambiguity is corrected not because it is threatening to the infant's life, but because it is threatening to the infant's culture" asserts social psychologist Suzanne Kessler.[14]

Culture is comfortable perceiving in two genders and assigning specific behaviors accordingly. However, nature itself has always presented us with more than the comfortable duality of male and female. According to Anne Fausto-Sterling, there are at least five sexes, with varying degrees of "male" or "female" characteristics. She perceives gender as "a vast, infinitely malleable continuum that defies the constraints of even five categories."[15] If gender were not determined by the surgeon's scalpel and culture's insistence to perceive dualistically, our world would reflect more diversity and less inhibition in regard to gender roles. By offering us various gender possibilities, nature seems to suggest that human experience is not limited to the gender roles assigned by culture.

It is a great challenge for most of us to imagine a world with more than two genders, one in which individuals develop themselves according to their inner natures. Opening up to ourselves in all of our great diversity and not letting gender define us helps alleviate sexism and homophobia. Sexism occurs when one gender insists, overtly or subtly, that his qualities are more valuable than hers and that his qualities are inaccessible to her. Sexism is a conscious or unconscious superiority backed by institutionalized power structures that uphold these gender divisions. Homophobia is a fear of intimacy between two people of the same gender and is often triggered in our society when any individual begins to explore himself outside of his cultural gender role.

Any attempt to attribute behavior to gender is a limitation of human development, making experience inaccessible to some. When such behaviors become structured in our educational, social, labor and political institutions, these then become limitations of human rights.

End Notes

[1] *The Oregonian,* June 30, 1991, L6.
[2] April Sinclair, *Ain't Gonna Be the Same Fool Twice* (New York: Avon Books, 1996) 171.
[3] *New York Times,* July 2, 1997: C9.
[4] *USA Today,* June 20, 1997: C1
[5] Women's Sports Foundation, *USA Today,* June 20, 1997: B1.
[6] For a complete discussion on edges and process theory see Arnold Mindell's *Working with the Dreaming Body* and *River's Way* (London: Routledge and Kegan Paul, 1985).
[7] Unfortunately in the middle of the 1998–99 season, the American Basketball League (ABL) declared bankruptcy, unable to compete with the financial backing and media contacts of the Women's National Basketball Association (WNBA).
[8] Rita Mae Brown, *Sudden Death* (New York: Bantam Books, 1984).
[9] This is the basic approach of process work. I am enormously grateful for Arnold Mindell's view of human nature and how he has modeled it in his own life and teachings as well as in his writing.
[10] Angela Davis, *Women, Race and Class* (New York: Vintage Books, 1983) 32, taken from the following sources: Barbara Ehrenreich, and Deirdre English, "Microbes and the Manufacture of Housework" *For Her Own Good: 150 Years of the Experts' Advice to Women* (Garden City, NY: Anchor Press/Doubleday, 1978); Ann Oakley, *Woman's Work: The Housewife Past and Present* (New York: Vintage Books, 1976); Eleanor Flexner, *Century of Struggle: The Women's Rights Movement in the U.S.* (New York: Atheneum, 1973); Mary P. Ryan *Womanhood in America* (New York: New Viewpoints, 1975).
[11] Davis 23.
[12] Davis 61. Taken from Elizabeth Cady Stanton, Susan B. Anthony, and Matilda Joslyn Gage, *History of Woman Suffrage* Vol. 1 (New York: Fowler and Wells, 1881), 115–117.
[13] Monika Bauerlein, "The Unkindest Cut" *Utne Reader* No. 77, October 1996.
[14] Bauerlein 16.
[15] Bauerlein 16, quoted from *The Sciences* (March/April, 1993).

Do You Think I'm Sexy?

As an adolescent I was convinced that I would never be sexy. Sexy was just not part of who I was. It was something to become, to strive for and attain, like a passing grade. Sexy was glamorous and trendy, reserved for the popular crowd. I watched with great insecurity as in-groups took enormous care in developing the styles, nuances and mannerisms that would make them appealing.

One afternoon, in the midst of my turbulent teenage years, my mother and I passed each other in the hallway. She flashed her usual look of disdain at my 70s high school garb of torn and patched jeans, flannel shirt and construction boots. Picking up the threads of a previous conversation she asked, "Don't you like it when men whistle at you in the street?" "No," I replied defensively and in disbelief that she was even asking me that question. "Do you?" I asked with equal contempt. Caught in a corner, she defended her position and admitted she liked the public attention, implying that any normal female would feel the same. Stunned and betrayed by her assertion, I flew into a rage. How could she enjoy being objectified and how could she suggest this to me, her daughter! It was as if she were telling me that my body didn't belong to me, but that its virtue lay only in the approval of anonymous men.

I have often wondered about that conversation. It puzzled me because of my mother's interest in the women's liberation movement. An attractive woman, my mother certainly didn't express her enjoyment at men's attention, but rushed by the leers and whistles as if they were daggers. It seemed utterly incongruous that my mother was encouraging me to revel in the attention of every Tom, Dick and Harry.

In fact, she wasn't, at least not consciously. She didn't want me to be objectified by men. It did not go along with her sophisticated demeanor and would embarrass her budding feminism. Rather, her comment was a desperate and provocative attempt to get me to emulate her sense of sex appeal and attraction. Indeed, throughout my childhood and adolescence the main battle between my mother and me centered around appearance. Some of my earliest memories about clothing involve squirming in discomfort from the itchiness of lace and synthetic fabrics, pulling on elastic that held me too tightly, and wanting to get out of patent-leather shoes that prevented me from walking comfortably. My mother thought such attire was appropriate and pretty. I preferred cottons and corduroys, loose-fitting clothes that felt snuggly and soft.

Although her persona prevented her from reveling in the attentions of anonymous men, I feel my mother spoke the truth in admitting that she enjoyed it. Like many women, my mother's sense of sex appeal lay in the visual appraisal of society's standards. Naturally, she wanted her daughter to reflect those same standards, which were the freeway to success in career, social life, marriage and self-esteem.

Although I fought her bitterly, I got the message early on; sexual appeal depended on cultural approval. Even as my generation tore down many taboos around sexuality and broke its puritanical silence, popular culture still defined what was sexy and what was not. Culture made it seem that people were either sexy or they weren't, that sexiness was a characteristic given to us just as our eye color. At the same time, advertising lured us into believing that we could be sexy if we only bought certain products, listened to popular music, reshaped our bodies and aped the gestures of glamorous stars.

Women coming of age in an atmosphere flooded with the visuals of trendy glamour and sellable-sex would need divine intervention to protect against the internal domination of such powerful and seductive cultural forces. How is a young woman to grow up discovering her unique sexual self when every woman and man around her is hypnotized by an outer image of sexiness? How can inner experience stand the onslaught of constant collective measurement?

I have never met a woman who is entirely free from the commercial image of female sexuality. Even those of us who are against it find ourselves entangled in its insidious web in that we are compelled to battle it. In our most private moments, the ever vigilant eye of commercial woman looks into our mirrors, disgusted and unhappy at the reflection, measuring, comparing and inspecting form, shape and size.[1]

When I was eighteen I drove a taxi cab for the summer. Not only was I the youngest driver on staff but I was the only woman, except for old Gertie, who had been driving forever. Gertie had her own car and regular fares, and therefore rarely had to subject herself to the group of hackers who hung out by the train station trying to hustle a fare. I was alone in a sea of lonely and hungry men. One hot and humid day while we waited for the commuter train to pull in to the station, one of the drivers looked me up and down and said "I like a woman with meat on her." I froze, not out of fear, but surprise. I looked up at him curiously. "White women are too skinny. I like something I can hold on to," he explained.

Even though I was clearly one of the skinny white women he was rejecting, I felt strangely complimented. I had never known a man to reject the commercialized skin-and-bones aesthetic of white women, although at that time I hadn't had many intimate conversations with black men or other men outside of white mainstream U.S. culture. As a relatively thin woman, hypnotized by the image of twiggy models, I still felt I wasn't thin enough. In a strange way his comments freed me, opened me to the possibility of a wider range of beauty, body image and sex appeal. It was the first time I had reflected on the dominance of white European standards of beauty and how they had completely permeated the consciousness of a diverse nation. This oppression spared no woman, but was totally annihilating for women of color. Despite the sexism in our interaction, I could appreciate that man for standing against mainstream standards of beauty and sex appeal, holding to his individual and cultural desires.

A couple years ago I was looking through some old photographs and came across a bunch from my twenties on a beach holiday. I surprised myself. I liked what I saw. I liked my body. I was shocked, and then disappointment and regret swept over me. I remember then doing the same thing I do now, looking in the mirror and rarely being satisfied, comparing myself to the commercial image of woman. I felt like I had missed the boat. The ideal that I was striving for was present then, but I couldn't see or appreciate it.

I could not see it because feeling attractive and sexy is not only a visual experience, as the fashion and sex industries would like us to believe. Many markets profit from selling the image of beauty and sex appeal, selling an image that few women will attain or feel inside that they have. Self-love cannot be sold—it is not a commodity. In fact, there is no real market on what is sexy and who can be sexy. Deep inside we all know this. At those moments when the flood of desire overwhelms and love glows from our pores, the haunting images of culture are washed away. It is then we know that sexiness is an inner feeling, an experience. When we strive to attain the commercial ideal we limit ourselves in our own experience.

Sexy is an experience, not a product. Recently, I saw a photograph of an eight-year-old female model made up and dressed in seductive women's clothing. I was repelled by the photo: the outer garments and adult poses she was imitating did not go along with her spirit.

When we feel connected to our inner spirit, to our spontaneous energies, emotions and authenticity, we are all irresistible. I was recently privy to a conversation between two men, a white man and a black man. The white man had just rejected a woman who had shown romantic interest in him. She was furious at him for superficially dismissing her, not seeing her spirit or acknowledging her as a sexual being, but quickly measuring her against the standards of so-called conventional beauty. The black man had witnessed what happened and later pulled the white man aside.

"You really missed an incredible woman," he said.

"Well, she just wasn't my type."

"Your type is all in your head. That's your problem. That woman had it. But you couldn't see it. She had what it takes, she is down. Didn't you see her dancing, the way she let herself go, she was connected."

I was stunned and intrigued by what I was hearing. The black man repeatedly challenged the white man's view of women. He would not let him off the hook and insisted that the white man's sexuality and feeling towards women were connected to an empty image of attraction that lacked soul. I felt privileged to hear the inside conversation between men, one that also crossed racial lines. It was refreshing to hear a man value a woman for her soul or inner radiation and not the visual aesthetic of her appearance.

If sex appeal is only visually oriented, then it is time limited. Collectively possessed by these visual images, our obsession with youth is pervasive. I remember a woman in her sixties at a seminar who felt compelled to introduce herself as a sexual being. She asserted that she felt overlooked and neglected in most groups and social situations in which she was seen as an asexual being, post menopausal and undesirable. The group loved her spontaneous outburst and hooted and hollered its approval.

Some years back I drew a portrait of my grandmother and presented it to her as a gift. I had drawn it from a recent photograph and felt she looked beautiful. Something from her soul radiated out from her gaze and possessed me. I worked for weeks on the drawing. When I finally presented it to her, I was not prepared for her response.

"Who is that old lady?" she asked.

"It's supposed to be you," I mumbled. Silence filled the room.

My grandfather strode over to the picture and began to critique the drawing. "There are too many wrinkles here. This line is not right there. She doesn't have that wrinkle."

I had naively stepped into a huge landmine. My eighty-five-year-old grandmother and grandfather were still connected to the image of a younger woman. They could not appreciate the beauty that I was seeing in her age.

Cultural definitions of what is sexy rarely reflect inner experience, which is limitless, free of mechanics and method and beyond the borders of age. Devoid of emotion and soul, the body, no matter how "beautiful" it is, seems like an empty vessel. It is our emotional and natural expression that brings sexual spirit to the body. If we ask ourselves what attracts us to our lovers, rarely is it simply a physical attribute, but the life and spirit that shine through that physical being. Often a gesture or twinkle or expression makes our heart rate quicken. Relationships that only value appearance lose their luster more quickly, as individuals do not develop the inner spirit inside of them. The cultural value placed on appearance makes sexuality a product and neglects inner experience. Relationship becomes a capitalistic venture motivated by the background drive for self-love, but disguised as ambition and gain. Who we love then reflects our self-esteem; our partners become trophies that elevate our own self worth.

I was in ninth grade, at a party, the new girl from the other side of town. The lights were low and young people huddled in groups or danced to the music. As I walked into the room I felt my skin crawling as eyeballs tracked my every move. I felt shy and uncomfortable, but excited and complimented as I noticed Daryl catch my eye and stride in my direction. Daryl was my age but had already filled out and looked as if he were a senior. He had the emotional confidence to match his body and was a popular boy to whom many girls were drawn. I gladly accepted his invitation to dance and thought that maybe this new school would be good for me. When the tune ended I thanked him and before I could even sit down, Lenny, a boy from my social studies class, was waiting for the next dance. Shocked and flattered by all the attention, I danced with Lenny. The evening went on as Daryl and Lenny traded dances with me. I was oblivious to the competition between them and the crowd of boys looking on. I was in a dream, reveling in attention that I never received in junior high school.

The romantic mood of "Color My World" permeated the atmosphere and dulled my street smarts; when the slow dance ended I enthusiastically agreed to Daryl's suggestion that we go outside for a walk. I wanted to know this boy whom I had been intermittently dancing with the last couple of hours. Who was he? Could I share my loneliness with him, did we have something in common? I was surprised when I found myself lying on the ground, his full weight on me, mouth pressed hard against mine. How does the body respond to conquest? I wasn't ready. My left leg kept rising towards my chest as I tried to lie back and relax, wanting him to like me. His mouth drilled into my face, drowning me with slobber. He was faceless and empty and treated me the same. I felt his hand move up my right side. Instinctually my right elbow clamped down tight against my skin. He pushed harder against my forearm and searched for an opening that would lead him to my breast. I carefully slid my left arm between the weight of our bodies and grabbed his wandering hand, hoping he would be content to hold my hand. He tired of me, got up, and said he was going inside. It was late and time to go. I walked past the group of boys and said goodbye to Daryl. He barely acknowledged my presence and the other boys laughed. On Monday morning I saw him in the school halls and he turned away from me.

I was a failed conquest and nothing more. I felt betrayed and foolish to be caught in my dreaming. How could I have missed the prevalence of conquest? Its effects were everywhere; it was the deed that was important, the product and whether it failed or succeeded. This drive to acquire and conquer has thoroughly marked our history. How could our adolescents be different? Conquest does not nurture experience, but orients us to the product or outcome. Sex becomes goal-oriented and individuals become points on a scoreboard. The means are overshadowed by the ends and relationship loses its vitality and dynamism as an experience. This has a great effect on our experience of sexiness. Relationship that values conquest over experience creates a market for sexy. It is no wonder that we orient ourselves to the material and commercial image of the sexy woman or man, cemented in youth, an image elevated by unconscious racism, material manipulation and select gene pools. What becomes of us when this fades? For those of us who never reach the goal or are never "acquired," what effect does this have on inner experience? Lastly, who is counting and what are we acquiring?

Buddhism would say that such striving and gathering is the background drive to enlightenment. After spending a life attached to the material plane and acquiring more and more, one is still empty, longing for enlightenment, or buddha nature. We are turned back onto ourselves, to find beauty and spirit in that which we have discarded, and to develop and embrace the living essence that we were each born with. The glow of life denies no child brought into this world. That glow is utterly attractive and, when nourished, flourishes into a spirit that is irrepressible. At the center of this glow lies the self-love and unique subjective experience of sexy. In that state the cultural hypnosis of appearance lifts its veil.

I remember when the spell of commercial sexuality began to loosen its grip from my mind. I was at a gathering and noticed a very large woman glowing with enthusiasm. Her intoxicating smile lit up the room. I noticed my attraction to her; I couldn't keep my eyes off her. Drawn into the sexy field around her, I was surprised to find myself engaged in a sexual fantasy. Since ordinarily I would have overlooked this woman, I was delighted to notice that my own inner values were changing and that the societal norm of what is sexy was losing its vise-like hold on me. At the same time I was pained to realize how many people I do dismiss or neglect based on my often unconscious views about appearance and sex appeal, ones that I also suffer from.

Sexy is an adventure, one that beckons us to explore what is behind the curtain, what is least known and therefore potentially transformational, stimulating and challenging to our core vitality. At times our relationships become more known and routine and we lose contact with the adventure and luminosity that first touched our hearts. For example, I remember working with two women in their fifties who wanted to explore the lack of sex in their relationship. They had been together twenty years. When I asked Sandy what turned her on to Vicki now or when they had first met, she said that it was Vicki's vulnerability that really drew her. Sandy described the experience in more depth as one in which Vicki was less sure of herself, more uncertain and spontaneous, emotional, and less predictable. Vicki piped up, "This is exactly what I struggle against. I don't want to be like that. I want to be strong and more certain." Vicki had a terrible abuse history, and showing any so-called vulnerability was dangerous to a part of her that had been badly hurt and hadn't been able to defend herself. Yet this was just the part of her that Sandy adored so much. The attraction lay in the fact that this state was less known, probably to both of them, and therefore held a world of numinous experience. When we protect each other's known worlds too much, we don't challenge each other in our own growth. Relationship then becomes more complacent and less sexy. To work at the edge of our known world and have the courage to explore new parts of ourselves is often frightening and shatters old patterns, but awakens us in new ways and stirs the spirit. This is the ultimate attraction!

Sexy is not a static experience, but continues throughout our lives in our desire to keep discovering and experiencing more of ourselves. Experience becomes lifeless when discovery stops. Obviously, sex appeal based on attaining a commercial model is time-limited. Sexy is spirit and resides in each of us. It is an inner experience that no one can define or contain, a radiation that irrepressibly draws, a zest for living fully that possesses us until our last days.

The growing spirit is a sexy one, free from the binds of consensus culture. I dream of a world in which we encourage our young people to believe in their inner experience and to develop their emotional and spiritual selves, rather than to mimic lifeless images of sexiness. We would raise a more diverse and openhearted population and give our children the greatest gift of all—self-love.

I still love soft fabrics and loose fitting clothing, tactile experiences that send me straight to heaven.

End Notes

[1] See Sara Halprin's *Look At My Ugly Face* (New York: Viking, 1995) for a revealing discussion about women's appearance.

Ode to Angela[1]

All the kids knew who Angela was and most of them kept their distance. I was afraid of her too. She was twice my size and the toughest girl in school, the only girl I knew who could beat up boys. She really commanded respect. Although we were the same age, Angela had been kept back a year, so I never saw her in any of my classes. I noticed her across the schoolyard, lingering alone in the bushes, beating someone up or holding court with a group gathered around her. I had my own group of girlfriends. Angela was someone to watch out for, to make sure I didn't cross her path.

When I was in the fourth grade we had our first personal encounter. We were in the schoolyard during lunch and the bell was about to call us back inside. Angela approached me to play "colors." Only a few of us girls collected baseball cards. Colors was a game in which a pile was created by each player putting down a card on top of the previous card. The team name on each card had a color. When one of your cards matched the color of the previous card, you would win the entire pile of cards.

I was afraid to begin playing right before the bell, knowing that once you started you couldn't stop until one person had no cards. Being late to school was not part of my identity. But Angela was insistent and I felt scared. We hunkered down next to the cool brick building and got serious. The more I won, the more terrified I became. Not only was I going to be late, but I was beating the toughest girl in the whole world. I was convinced she was going to kill me. Since this game depended on luck, I couldn't even throw the game. There were other games that had to do with flipping and knocking down cards that were propped up against a wall; at least with these games I could lose on purpose and save my life.

The next thing I remember was running wildly back to class with a stack of cards in my coat pocket.

Weeks later I somehow found myself standing in the bushes with Angela and her gang. I obviously didn't belong. I wasn't Italian and I wasn't Catholic and I was about to get the shit beat out of me. To my surprise, Angela stood in front of me. Alone, she prevented a whole group from tearing me apart.

My next meeting with Angela didn't occur until years later in junior high school. We sat next to each other in chorus, enjoying the same songs. Carole King's album "Tapestry" had just come out and we walked outside, screeching "I feel the earth move under my feet...." These moments of friendship were few. We came from different worlds, with some unspoken rule that our paths should never really cross.

Silver Lake had a reputation as a tough small town where first, second and third generation Italian Americans defended their turf and way of life. There were three Jewish kids in my grade besides me and a few kids who were Protestant. St. Anthony's was right down the street, and all social life was organized through the church and local Catholic organizations. I was not merely an outsider; by the time I was twelve I was fighting daily for my survival against blatant anti-Semitism.

Angela must have had her own troubles. Although a key figure in the higher echelons of the Silver Lake gangs, she seemed awfully alone. Everyone knew and respected her, but no one was truly close to her. Angela was tough, loud, physically imposing, and heavyset, not the kind of conventionally attractive girl who drew others to her. She was abrasive, always ready for a fight and often getting in trouble with authorities.

Music brought us together, crossing cultural and ethnic boundaries, but that didn't happen until years later in high school. We strummed out simple chords and sang beautiful harmonies to the introspective and political tunes of the early 1970s. High school was larger and a little more diverse. We benefited from some of the liberal curriculum changes of the time. Humanities classes included social issues, women's studies, political movements and history. These put us in closer contact with the spirit of the songs we sang, expanding our views of ourselves and the confining town in which we lived.

Angela began to attend my humanities and women's studies classes. She was a grade behind me and tracked in different classes. Most of her educational history had been spent going to as few classes as possible, so it was quite a shock to see her going to classes she was not registered for. We'd pass each other in the halls. She'd yell, "See you in class," and I knew which class she meant. This class was team taught. We had never met teachers who invited us to call them by their first names, cursed, and spoke openly about sexuality. They challenged the way we saw the world by their own behavior and brought in ideas outside the borders of Silver Lake. The radical zeitgeist of the early 1970s was seeping into the schools of small town U.S.A.

Something was happening to Angela. I had never seen her excited about learning. The old Silver Lake gang began to keep their distance and told her she should stop hanging out with her "Jew friends," hippies and freaks. She brushed off hurtful comments and held strongly to her new interests and friendships. Despite our new connection, I think I only saw the inside of her home a couple of times, and she only came to my house a few times. Bridging our worlds in high school was no less difficult than in junior high. My parents looked down on her and hers did the same to me. Our friendship blossomed in school, in the streets, in cars, and in the woods.

The early 70s were exciting for adolescent young women. The women's movement was in full force, and Title IX was passed, demanding equality in schools for girl's activities and sports programs. Female sexuality was shedding its shackles, pushing out of its culturally defined limitations. Many women from my generation lost our virginity without thinking of ourselves as "whores," "sluts" or "loose." Many of us dared to conflict with the beauty myth, wore our jeans and flannel shirts proudly, threw our bras to the winds and let our body hair be.

We all pushed limits with our parents, but Angela's struggle seemed more burdened than my own. I knew I would get out of this town, that my ideas and impulses had a future. I knew there was a world where I could live all I was learning about and fighting for. I would leave home and go to college. I think for a time Angela actually felt she could get out. She refused to serve her father and brothers and began to stand for her dreams of living a life outside Silver Lake. She even thought she might attend college. In her traditional Italian family the roles of daughters and sons were laid in stone. No one left the family; no one even left the town. Even though Silver Lake was a 35 minute train ride to New York City, no one ventured out.

Angela's troubles became more severe. The higher her spirits, the more oppression this constellated at home. I wanted to save her and I knew that according to her mother I was part of the problem. In my teenage naïveté I thought I could help her. If I loved her enough, encouraged her enough, helped her find scholarships and financial aid, she just might have a chance. My own privileges blinded me to the complexities of the social issues Angela was dealing with. I sensed my privileges in my own embarrassment and discomfort about the future. I felt shy to admit that I would go to college, that my parents could afford to help me with tuition, and that I had the freedom to dream of other lifestyles. It is a privilege to know that you can leave home and that your parents want you to. My parents saw the times changing and knew that I would go my own way regardless of how much they protested. Angela's parents kept to their old world views and enforced them with physical abuse. I could see the jealousy of generations of women holding her back, not allowing her to do things that they could never dream of. As a matter of fact, I saw that happen to many of the girls in my town, girls who had hope, vision, and intelligence. I watched them gradually trade in their independence and self-determination for the security of collective approval.

In early Spring during our junior year, Angela hadn't attended school for a couple of days, so I called her up. "My father died," she said quite lightly. "Will you be at the funeral?" St. Anthony's was crowded and the Latin chants and heavy incense transported me to another world. Angela seemed strangely detached, waiting for it all to end. Some family and friends commended her for her strength and others attacked her for her lack of feeling. At last alone, she confided to me that she wouldn't miss him. At times she had wished him dead, wanting to free herself from the senseless brutality of a disturbed man.

Angela was not mourning and her mother didn't like it. Her newfound excitement flourished and we talked for hours about our latest ideas and discoveries. Angela's mother thought this sacrilegious and blamed Angela for her new interests. I became more frightened to call her home and never went inside when I went to pick her up. Angela became zealous about losing weight. Amphetamines helped curtail her appetite and gave her lots of energy to exercise. Her enthusiasm for learning and new relationships continued. One of those relationships was with Ms. B., a teacher who encouraged her learning.

One day after school we went to Angela's house. No one else was home. I felt uncomfortable, knowing I wasn't really welcome. My uneasiness grew when the lights went out suddenly. We were in the basement and Angela had turned the lights out. She searched for me in the dark. My heart beat rapidly and I yelled for her to put the lights back on. I felt something strange happening and began to search for the door. I told her that she was scaring me and I wanted to leave. She said she wanted to kiss me and she'd turn on the lights if I let her. I followed the walls in the dark, dank room, hoping to feel a doorknob. Suddenly Angela was upon me, kissing me. I struggled to get out from under her. "Okay, now let me go!" I screamed, scrambling to my feet. She turned on the lights and I fled outside.

I needed to go home where I was expected for dinner. I had just gotten my driver's license and had my parent's car. Walking to the car, I realized that my jacket and keys were inside Angela's house. As I walked back, Angela sauntered out, dangling the keys before me. She closed them in her fist, saying she wouldn't give them to me unless I kissed her. I screamed at her to give me the keys and let me go home. I was already late; it was getting dark, and my parents were going to be angry. She came after me, pinned me against the fence, pressed herself against me and tried to kiss my neck. I thrashed out wildly, trying to get away. She slapped me across the face, and in the struggle the keys fell to the ground and I grabbed them. I ran frantically to the car and she followed. Each time I attempted to open the door she pushed herself in the car with me. It seemed to take forever to get myself in the car with the doors locked. Finally, I could go home.

But Angela became more desperate and more reckless. She jumped on top of my parents' car and pounded on the roof. Then she took a huge stone, smashed it down on the roof, glued herself to the windshield and dared me to drive. By this time I was hysterical. Tears of hurt, anger, and desperation rolled down my face. Something had flipped in Angela. I felt like a trapped animal willing to do anything for my survival. I slowly began to back the car out of her driveway, hoping she would jump off, but she clung to the windshield wipers. I opened the window and told her to get off the car. She refused and again I felt cornered.

I drove up her street to the stop sign, all the while honking my horn and yelling for her to get off. She didn't move and pleaded with me to let her in the car. I felt terrified, praying for her to get off the hood before I turned onto the main road. She wouldn't move, and in my own panic I turned left on Lake Street with Angela hanging on the hood. I honked my horn, hoping someone would come out and help. After driving about a third of a mile I realized she would not move and could really get hurt. I pulled into a local Italian restaurant and leaned down on my horn. The waiters came out and laughed at the sight of Angela hanging on my car. I pleaded with them to get her off, but Angela knew everyone. She addressed them all by name, telling them to go inside, that everything was all right. I was shocked and incredulous that they did nothing despite the fact that I was crying and screaming. Finally, a police car drove up and Angela jumped off the car. They sent me home while Angela pleaded with me to take her home too. The police asked about the damage to the car and I told them to forget it, that Angela should go home too.

I was crying and shaking when I arrived home, terrified at having to explain the damage to the car and consequently reveal the whole story. The next day at school I felt dazed and tried to keep a safe distance from Angela, who searched for me throughout the day. At the end of Ms. B's class, she found me and lunged towards me. She chased me through the maze of chairs and desks until Ms. B. came between us. Ms. B. talked to us each separately. I broke down and confided in her. She told Angela to give me some time and space. I was afraid of Angela, but I also wanted to maintain our friendship and didn't want to reject her.

Angela's extreme state unfolded in the following days. She was found naked and disoriented in a deserted lot close to her house. At home she shocked her family by sprawling naked on the living room couch, publicly removing her tampon and throwing it in the air. She then threw used tampons and sanitary napkins all over the house and refused to put her clothes on. Another day she was found jogging naked on a busy highway. The next thing I knew she had been institutionalized and I was fighting the authorities to allow me to bring her guitar to her.

I visited her regularly despite the negative vibes from my parents and her mother. For some strange reason I remained oddly detached from our incident. I saw it as part of a larger process she was involved in. I missed her friendship and spent many hours wondering what had happened to her. Although I knew nothing about extreme states, I developed my own theory. My teenage brain concluded that the world of her conventional family had no room for all of her dreams and passion. She couldn't deal with the tension between the two worlds and she cracked.

Even back then I knew that culture and extreme states were somehow connected, although I couldn't have said how until I learned through my studies in process work. I was convinced that if Angela had had support for her deepest nature she wouldn't have gone "crazy." What I didn't see at that time was the meaningfulness of her extreme behavior, not only for herself but for the collective around her.

Angela was one of many women trying to be herself in the midst of cultural oppression. Even though there was a national trend towards women's liberation and progressive education, Silver Lake remained as conventional as old Italy. Angela's story reflects the stories of many women who have had to become extreme to break out of terribly oppressive conventions. Often when women have dared to do this, they have been institutionalized.

Women and "Mental Illness"

Statistically, more women than men have been institutionalized for mental illness.[2] In *Women's Madness: Misogeny or Mental Illness?*, Ussher asserts that such statistics are not due to the female gender being more prone to mental illness, but result from a worldwide cultural history oppressive to women.[3] She says:

> ...misogynistic practices are construed as analogous to the discourse of madness, in that they act to contain us, and as a part of the constrictions which lead to madness itself because they create a culture of incarceration and oppression within which madness is the inevitable outcome for women.[4]

Angela dared to venture out of her role as a daughter, whose sole purpose was to be subservient, find a husband, and have a family. The history of marriage is not based on the dream of romantic love and partnership, but on ownership; women as property, owned by men.[5] Chesler postulates that many women have gone "insane" to avoid marriage and the conventional lifestyle expected of them. Therefore, the following statistics come as no surprise:

- Women who rejected the domestic role have a higher chance of rehospitalization.
- Female schizophrenics conformed the least to social roles, even as children.
- A 1958 study confirms that when people act outside of their gender roles they are more subject to hospitalization. Ussher's more recent research confirms these findings as well.
- Lesbians are committed at earlier ages than heterosexual women and are kept three times as long in institutions.[6]
- Less educated and more 'attractive' women are probably released sooner and more easily from state hospitals and from private treatment.[7]
- In 1964 the number of American women involved in the psychiatric system began to dramatically increase.[8]
- Sixty-nine percent of suicide attempts are by women.[9]

Angela became one of these statistics. As she remained in the hospital, I sadly watched her spirit die. Her enthusiasm for life and learning vanished; even music held little interest. Her eyes glazed over and she seemed to move through a haze. Heavily medicated, she became disoriented and emotionless. She didn't relate to anyone, even to those of us who had been close friends. She looked defeated and empty, and I mourned the loss of a friend and a great spirit. Visitors were forbidden for a period of time; finally I got to see her again. Upon arriving I discovered that she had been given a series of electroshock treatments.[10] I felt horrified and saddened. Angela had become a zombie, a human being with no personality, no color, walking aimlessly through the corridors. I couldn't reach her. She was gone. They had crushed her spirit, her music, her zest for life and our friendship. I too was defeated. At sixteen, I felt powerless to interact with the system that had done this.

The doctors and her mother all said this treatment was for her own good. They saw it as therapeutic; with time she would be released and lead a "normal" life. They expected her to be able to hold down a job with minimal stress and intellectual requirements and to develop a social life through which she would eventually meet the man of her dreams and settle down. Ussher questions for whom such treatment is therapeutic. She asserts that this kind of treatment does not serve the needs of the women themselves, but is meant to maintain the dominant societal order.[11] In my opinion, this treatment certainly did not serve Angela.

City Shadows: Honoring Angela

Mindell's central contribution to the field of psychiatry postulates the concept of a "city shadow," which furthers our understanding of so-called psychotic or extreme states and their relationship to the collective. Mindell adopted the neutral term "extreme state" in order to show that certain states are deemed "psychotic," "crazy" or "insane" relative to the cultural norm. The word extreme implies that these states occur relatively infrequently for a given culture. Thus the dominant culture has difficulty understanding them and considers them unacceptable.[12] In her historical review of women's madness, Ussher sees this similarly. She asserts that "madness is not an illness but a social construction."[13] Chesler proposes that:

> Men are generally allowed a greater range of "acceptable" behaviors than are women. It can be argued that psychiatric hospitalization or

> labeling relates to what society considers "unacceptable" behavior. Thus, since women are allowed fewer total behaviors and are more strictly confined to their rolesphere than men are, women, more than men, will commit more behaviors that are seen as "ill" or "unacceptable."[14]

Mindell demonstrates that the individual in an extreme state is a city shadow, displaying behavior that goes against the collectively accepted consensus of the norm. This individual acts like a dream figure for the collective, embodying behavior split off from mainstream consciousness. Mindell explains:

> This shadow is like the city's dream portraying its neglected gods, the hopelessness it will not admit, its withdrawal from superficial communication, its suicidal tendencies, mania, addictions, murderous rage and hypersensitivity. The shadow reminds us of the smoldering revolution we normally perceive only in the dark of night or in the impinging quality of physical symptoms.[15]

I had always seen Angela's "odd" behavior as a manifestation of the terrible social and inner pressures she was under. However, I want to honor her here by acknowledging her as a city shadow for the town we grew up in, the school we went to, the families we came from, and the larger world around us. Her extreme state is a collective dream, a message for us all. We are the dreamers challenged to grow.

When I began to research women's extreme states relative to culture, I found numerous cross-cultural taboos regarding women's behavior. Most of these are associated with the body, sexuality, reproduction and menstruation.[16] There are volumes of study on this topic; I offer a few tidbits.

Ussher offers a brief history of the menstrual taboo. Women have been seen as contaminated and unclean when menstruating, barred from worship and work. A man who risks sexual intercourse with a menstruating woman could become impotent or brain damaged. Women are thought not to be able to think clearly when they have their periods. A menstruating woman could cause crops to fail or fruit to rot.[17] These beliefs might seem outdated to the modern reader: however, menstruation is still used as an excuse that women cannot perform as well as men in the workplace. Women's emotions, moods and ideas are often dismissed and not valued during menstruation. Pre-menstrual Syndrome (PMS) can be used as a medical way to further categorize and dismiss women. Additionally, the sense of being dirty is still with us, whether as an attitude held by men or internalized by women themselves.

Women have been seen as sexually out of control if left on their own and have been kept under lock and key with chastity belts. Cultural morality has held the keys to women's virginity. Openly sexual women were accused of being witches. Chinese women endured foot binding so they would be more sexually attractive to men.[18] Millions of females worldwide succumb to genital mutilation; one of the background myths is that if the female genitals are left intact they will grow down to the women's knees and make them sexually ravenous.[19] Lesbian sexuality has been taboo throughout the ages; these women have been viewed as witches or pathologized and incarcerated.[20] Homosexuality remains illegal in many parts of the world.

Ancient and modern practices which denigrate the female body and control female sexuality are central to misogyny. Cross-culturally, generations of women have existed solely to please others. These misogynist attitudes have seeped into the female psyche, tarnished self-esteem and encouraged self-hatred. Women feel torn, longing for love and acceptance for their innate selves, while they simultaneously strive to achieve the cultural female ideal by inhibiting and molding themselves into the culturally acceptable female form.

Angela was caught in this vicious struggle. She broke familial and cultural rules and simultaneously fanatically exercised and starved herself to attain the norm. Like most women, she was split between embracing mainstream ideals and fighting against them. In her extreme state the cultural chains were broken and everything forbidden was released. In a culture that shamed her for her heavy body, wanting her to hide her flesh and disguise her appearance, she stripped naked. In a culture that is repulsed by women's menses and that teaches us ultimate discretion during these periods, Angela acted flamboyant, rambunctiously forcing us to notice a natural female beauty. In the extreme state, the naked woman in her natural state is unearthed.

Angela's behavior also broke relationship taboos. In a world that condemns same gender love, in a country where the highest teenage suicide rate occurs amongst gay teenagers,[21] and in North American high schools where the nastiest insult is to call someone "queer," "fag," or "dyke," Angela dared to express her desires.

In a world that has been so unconscious in the area of relationship and sexuality, relationships have been monitored for all kinds of potential abuse. Therefore, when Angela gave Ms. B. a Mother's Day card with her deeply expressed sentiments, Ms. B. blamed herself. She felt she should have remained more distant and abruptly pulled away from Angela. Such relationship regulation spoils spontaneous and life-transforming relationship contacts. Angela broke this taboo as well, seeing correctly that Ms. B. mothered her more than her own mother did.

Angela also broke the convention around mourning her deceased father. She felt incredible pressure to grieve and many people in her environment criticized her distant demeanor. Beneath her coolness lived years of pain and fury from being hurt and mistreated. If she had been able to totally throw off the chains of social convention, perhaps she would have celebrated, free at last from a man who had never been fatherly.

Mainstream thinking is zealously moral about relationships, regulating the kinds of relationships and behavior it deems acceptable. Angela's state gave us a glimpse of a world in which nature or spirit creates relationship life, not humans or morals. Nature draws us to someone regardless of their gender, position in society, or racial and ethnic background. These are matters of the heart, not of laws or morality.

Extreme States and the Mainstream

Extreme states remain difficult for the mainstream not only because they threaten basic cultural beliefs and norms, but because they generally manifest themselves with little regard for mainstream feedback. There is usually little interaction around the extreme state. Fear and shock result in mainstream withdrawal and rejection. We often feel threatened by the unusual state and try to stop it, unable to appreciate and unfold its inherent intelligence and meaning. Such fear also indicates our lack of familiarity with our own altered states of consciousness.

In the acute phase of Angela's extreme state, she no longer adapted herself to the behavioral expectations of the mainstream. Her inability to pick up feedback from the environment and adjust her behavior accordingly allowed her to live her dreaming process completely. Mindell states that not picking up feedback is not a pathological feature but can be observed in each of us at one time or another. We become unconscious of outer phenomena

> in order to preserve and complete the inner story or myth [we] are working on. In other words, having no feedback loop functions to

keep [us] in [our] own dream world, and this is a function of unconsciousness which can be observed in all of us.[22]

Since we all have difficulties relating to our own extreme and unconscious states, we lack the ability to relate to others in those states.

Mindell has demonstrated that when we experience an extreme state, we lack a feedback loop and cannot metacommunicate about our experiences. The lack of a metacommunicator, a part of the person that is able to meta-comment on experiences as they occur, over an extended period of time is a central aspect of extreme states. Mindell describes a feedback loop as what occurs when an individual adjusts her behavior to the opinions, expectations and signals coming from the environment. A missing feedback loop can be another characteristic of extreme states; this lack of outer adaptation enables the individual to remain in her inner process. The identity which normally adapts to outer feedback is not accessible. There is little regard for what were once personal or collective edges. This disregard allows new parts of ourselves to emerge. Not in contact with the edges of her identity, meaning collective norms and her own personal inhibitions, Angela temporarily lived parts of herself otherwise forbidden. Not only did she step into the dreaming world of her own personal psychology, but her behavior was a dream for her environment as well. Extreme states such as Angela's portray the dreaming drama of a given culture, showing us our own collective conflicts by revealing that which we disavow.[23]

Angela was not able to pick up my negative feedback to her advances and I was not able to relate to the shadow she revealed. I can only praise her now for carrying the ghost of an irrepressible woman and having the soul to tread unknown land in a town that stood against her, in an environment that eventually destroyed her spirit. But the essence of that spirit can never be destroyed. It is the eternal spirit of Kali, the mythical goddess of Indian culture, dancing and celebrating her innate female pleasures and furiously stomping the collective which has downed her.[24] Her spirit is evoked today throughout the world as women struggle, not only within the psychiatric system, but as all of us try to live our most genuine inner natures. This is liberation for women and for men—a human liberation, free from culturally induced roles. Angela takes her place among centuries of women who have foreshadowed this revolution, blazing the trail for many of us to come. I pay homage to them all.

End Notes

[1] First published as "Madness as Feminism," in *The Journal of Process Oriented Psychology* (Portland, OR: Lao Tse Press, 1994) Vol. 6, No. 1.
[2] Phyllis Chesler, *Women and Madness* (Garden City, NY: Doubleday, 1972). Also see Jane Ussher, *Women's Madness: Misogyny or Mental Illness?* (Amherst, MA: University of Massachusetts Press, 1992) for information on recent studies in Britain, Europe and the United States which confirm these statistics. Ussher refers to studies that indicate that women are referred more frequently for mental health services than are men. Psychotropic drugs are prescribed for women twice as frequently as they are for men, and more women receive ECT (electro-convulsive therapy, or electroshock).
[3] Chesler.
[4] Chesler 20.
[5] Chesler 20.
[6] Chesler 20.
[7] Chesler 69. From W.R. Orr, Ruth Anderson, Margaret Martin Des. F. Philpot, "Factors Influencing Discharge of Female Patients from a State Mental Hospital," *American Journal of Psychiatry,* Vol. 3, 1954.
[8] Chesler 69. I think this was due to the zeitgeist, the beginnings of the women's liberation and civil rights movement; a time when many women began to conflict with their limited roles and began to seek psychiatric help for their unhappiness.
[9] Chesler 69.
[10] Ussher presents various studies showing that ECT is more widely prescribed for women than men (108). From her footnotes: "Malla (1988) in a study which examined 5,729 psychiatric admissions over three years Reported that the 1,236 patients who received ECT were more likely to be female and older than the patients who received other treatments. Breggin (1979) reported that 80% of patients who receive ECT in one USA Hospital are women, because its disabling effects are deemed less problematic in women.": 124.
[11] Ussher.
[12] Arnold Mindell, *City Shadows: Psychological Interventions in Psychiatry* (London and NY: Routledge, 1988).
[13] Ussher: 1992, 166). Mindells's ideas about the city shadow also find support from those in the so-called "antipsychiatry" movement. Ussher presents such theories as Scheff and Goffman who argue that "...all madness is dependent on social and cultural values, not scientific objectivity. Psychiatry is thus seen as an agent of social control" (1992: 135). She also presents various authors who assert that pathological behavior has a definite cultural bias and gives examples of how definitions of madness are inconsistent between various cultures and societies. (135; 138).
[14] Chesler, 1972: 39ff.
[15] Mindell, 1988: 162.

[16] Ussher, 1992.
[17] Ussher. See also Lara Owen, *Her Blood is Gold: Celebrating the Power of Female Menstruation* (San Francisco: Harper, 1993).
[18] Chesler and Ussher.
[19] Alice Walker and Pratibha Parmar, *Warrior Marks: Female Genital Mutilation and the Sexual Blinding of Women* (New York: Harcourt, 1993).
[20] Ussher.
[21] A study compiled by the Hetrick Martin Institute in New York in 1992 revealed that gay teenagers are two to three times more likely to commit suicide than heterosexual teens. The Secretaries Task Force on Youth Suicide at the Department of Human Services in 1989 also reported similar findings.
[22] Arnold Mindell, *City Shadows*: 39.
[23] Mindell, *City Shadows*. See Chapter 3 for a deeper theoretical discussion about metacommunication, feedback loops and the connection between extreme states and field theory.
[24] Felix Guirand ed., *The New Larousse Encyclopedia of Mythology,* (New York: Hamlyn, 1959) and J. Hoch-Smith and A. Spring eds. *Women in Ritual and Symbolic Roles* (New York: Plenum, 1978).

"Am I Really?"

"Does this mean I'm *really* a lesbian?" the woman whispered in a cracked voice. She looked around nervously, afraid that someone would hear, or worse yet, confirm the ominous truth that lay naked in her question.

Ironically, many of us heard her. She had just revealed her deepest fear and curiosity to 200 people who had gathered for a seminar on group work, diversity issues and conflict resolution. This afternoon we were focusing on homosexuality and homophobia.

Olga was a woman in her late thirties from Germany. She was married and had several children. She had traveled alone from Germany to the seminar. I don't know what moved her to speak; after tumultuous conflict the group had come to a point where individuals were addressing the personal aspects of their own homophobia. This was the first time she had spoken in the large group.

I studied her carefully, her desperation and panic, her confusion and need to know what her sexual fantasies and fleeting feelings for other women meant. Suddenly I was propelled back in time, remembering myself at age twenty. I was in a relationship with a man I loved when I began having those same fleeting attractions to women. I too, wondered what they meant. In my attempt to understand something "forbidden" which would destroy my cozy heterosexual picture of reality, I, too, approached these feelings analytically. I searched for reasons and tried to put my feelings in some perspective from the world that I knew. The world around me deemed such feelings as abnormal and until I went to college I knew no one who was gay, lesbian, or bisexual.

Thou Shalt Not Deviate

Cultural difference is often equated with pathology. Experiences outside the norm are usually not greeted with discovery and wonder, but with disdain and fear. These visceral and subjective feeling reactions constitute the emotional basis of pathological thinking. Unable to explore and celebrate difference, we quickly condemn it, hoping we can isolate and restrain it, fearing it might spread.

Pathological thinking compels us to wonder what our feelings mean. Without it, we are fluid feeling beings. When we are happy we don't usually question why. We enjoy it. When a man and a woman are attracted to each other, they don't wonder if they are *really* heterosexual, nor do they question the meaning of their sexual feelings.

When we wonder about the meaning of our feelings and attractions, we are saying that they do not fit into our known range of experience. We examine ourselves, trying to conceptualize how our experiences might fit into our known worlds. If we conclude that they don't belong, how do we evaluate them? Without support or role models, it is all too easy to either deny experience or pathologize ourselves. These are the seeds of internalized homophobia, sexism, racism, and so forth. We begin to hate our inner lives and to view ourselves through the same lens as homogeneous culture that disavows and denounces difference.

When I was twenty, my interest in personal growth, coupled with the negative climate around homosexuality, led me to conclude that I was going through a phase and I would eventually grow out of it. My psychological observations, confirmed readily in my environment, compelled me to see my experiences as pathological. After all, describing love as a "phase" does not exactly encourage relationship; rather it is a psychologically sophisticated means of minimizing experience. Inadvertently, my strong drive for self discovery was used against me as I strove to understand fragile feelings in a pathological framework. I had little awareness of the subtle self-hatred that such thinking fosters.

In my early twenties I was looking for support and role models. I was studying psychology in Switzerland with a small learning community. I looked up to a group of women about ten years older than I, and I was shy and nervous about how my female lover and I would be received by this group. I felt like an oddity; a freak with problems, yet an exotic curiosity.

These women were all married to men, yet a strong bond electrified the atmosphere between them. They taunted and teased each other, flirting with the background sexuality between them. As they shared their dreams and feelings about each other with me, I began to feel less like an outsider. I felt their fascination with my relationship and welcomed it naïvely as an interest in me.

Many times I heard these women say, "I do have dreams and feelings about sleeping with women, but I don't have to act on them." I questioned myself, "Why do I have to act on my feelings? Maybe one day I will learn more about myself and I won't have to act on them either." Being young, trusting and desperate, I didn't realize the subtle condescension or perceive the elusive exploitation. I didn't question those whom I was looking up to, but doubted myself.

I don't think those women were intentionally malicious, just terribly unconscious. They didn't realize how they flirted with their own homosexuality through my experiences. They didn't see how their declaration to not act on their sexual impulses inadvertently pathologized my own.

Sex-Bashing

These generally open-minded women, interested in the diversity of human experience, represent a large portion of the mainstream. This "liberal" section of society votes in favor of human rights legislation and against the strong tide of anti-gay rights bills presently sweeping the United States. This liberal voice says that everyone is equal and should have the right to pursue their own happiness freely. However, this same voice is uncomfortable when its own sexuality stirs in the direction of someone of the same gender. It wonders "why," and the analytical process begins, reducing experience to pathology or insignificance. This is the root of how we begin to pathologize difference. When we marginalize aspects of our own sexuality, we unconsciously oppress parts of ourselves and others. We enforce the dominant social belief that says homosexuality is an inferior experience.

Marginalizing and categorizing our own sexuality inadvertently creates an open playing field for the introduction of anti-gay rhetoric and legislation. If gay-bashing happens intra-psychically, how could it not occur outwardly? Any time we put down experience without openly exploring it, we bash ourselves. And when we put down experience in ourselves, we help sustain norms that subtly or not so subtly stigmatize behavior. The stigma of abnormality will remain glued to homosexuality until we are able to fluidly explore sexuality.

The political far right knows this, and therefore claims that there is a massive gay movement trying to recruit our children. These paranoid rantings strike fear in the heart of the mainstream. However, the far right *does* accurately see that gay and bisexual relationships are becoming more public. The growing exposure of various relationship possibilities is beginning to create an encouraging climate, in which both adolescents and adults can explore their sexual selves. This is the larger threat: normalization. Active recruiting of children or anyone can be quickly silenced, disregarded as extreme or fanatic. However, lifting the stigma of abnormality would foster inner freedom and create an environment where a variety of relationships and lifestyles co-exist without external condemnation.

Relationship Is Not a Multiple Choice Test

Was Adrianne *really* a lesbian? This was one of the sub-themes in the 1995–96 season on *NYPD Blue,* a popular U.S. weekly television drama series. Adrianne's male co-detective had been coming on to her, so she declared herself a lesbian. For a couple of weeks this explained to the national television audience and the TV characters why Adrianne was not responding to Detective Martinez's advances. It also made for juicy gossip at the 15th precinct and elicited the usual displays of cruelty and homophobia.

Just as everyone was wondering who Adrianne's female lover was, she dropped a bombshell. No, she didn't think she was *really* a lesbian; she only said it because she couldn't turn Martinez down. In fact, she then revealed that because all of her relationships with men had been awful, she was considering that she might be a lesbian. The story-line for this mainstream television drama continued predictably when Adrianne trusted Martinez and they began an intimate relationship.

ABC network television thought it was on the edge with its introduction of a "gay" theme. However, there was nothing new or revolutionary presented here; just the same old mainstream thinking where homosexual love emerges as a pathological substitute. If ABC had shown Adrianne's desires and her struggle in having intimate feelings for women within a culture that evaluates these feelings as pathological, that would have been radical and deep. But there was not a hint of Adrianne's feelings or sexual desires. Her idea about being a lesbian had nothing to do with her inner feeling, but was a rational deduction based on "her" failure in relationships with men.

The desire to be sexual with someone of the same gender is not a substitute experience. Having bad relationships has to do with relating, not with gender. Being attracted to someone has to do with feeling and chemistry, not with appraisals and calculations. Attractions are not surrogates, and relationship is not a multiple-choice test.

In Search of the Elusive Cause

Determining whether one can *really* be gay is a cultural obsession. Researchers as well as the layperson are fascinated with pinpointing the *cause* of homosexuality. Over the years research has confirmed every hypothetical theory; culture, family, psychology, the environment, biology and genetics have all been "proven" as etiological factors. Simultaneously, tests in recent years show none of these factors are conclusive. In 1973 the American Psychiatric Association (APA) removed homosexuality from its list of pathological disorders. Despite removing the diagnosis, the APA acknowledged that there is still considerable controversy over whether homosexuality per se is a mental disorder.

The search for a cause continues; in the labs, in political discourse, in our bedrooms, and in our minds. Every time we question whether we are *really* gay or straight, and each time we disavow our sexual experiences and try to categorize them, we are the researchers viewing our most intimate experiences of love through the biased lens of cultural disapproval.

The need to pinpoint a cause is due to the intense fear of "catching it." No one researches the causes of heterosexuality except to understand why people deviate from that norm. If we know the cause we can treat it. Like a virus, we can develop a vaccine and prevent it. Many wish for the discovery of a biological cause so they could claim homosexuality is natural. I can understand and appreciate this desire. However, just because something is proven to be inherently biological does not mean society will not interfere in nature's creation and elicit medical, social or psychological intervention. The desire from many in the gay world to pinpoint a "gay" gene is due to the need for unwavering support, a defense made in heaven, stemming from the natural world.

The need for a divine defense becomes crucial in an atmosphere loaded with the religious absolutism of fundamentalist thought. From the viewpoint of the religious right no one is naturally gay; homosexuality is a dangerous and sinful behavior, a willful choice, an addiction that must be overcome. Absolutist thought is very seductive; it makes us think that the world is ordered and that there is a permanence to experience. It is the absolutist in each of us who searches for a set identity and disavows experience that does not go along with it. And it is the absolutist who unconsciously becomes self-righteous and insists on that identity for everyone.

Am I really…? is a question that searches for absolutes, a fixed answer, hoping to secure an identity. It is a question stemming from fear; fear of uncertainty and fear of experiencing that which is collectively held in contempt. When we ask *"Am I really?…"* we are in danger of exploring ourselves through the lens of pathology where experience becomes static, isolated, named and filed. When we inquire about our sexuality with the intent to secure a fixed identity, we freeze experience and lose our freedom to explore and dream, to develop by going into worlds that we don't know. The label and identity become more important than our actual experience. The label then reflects a hierarchy of experience or identities. The highest identity in the current sexual identity hierarchy is heterosexuality. This hierarchy is apparent even in the most well-meaning and open-minded individuals. It is apparent in each of us when we evaluate what we *really* are.

Nature's Work Has No Name

A friend recently told me her mother phoned to tell her that her cousin just came out. This "liberal" mother, who knows some gay people, shared the news as if she were announcing a death. My friend was delighted to hear about the recent development in her family and enthusiastically congratulated her mother. The mother was taken aback and wondered how her daughter could be so happy; "It will be so hard for him," the mother lamented.

This good-hearted woman is against discrimination. She holds ideals of an open and diverse world, yet she announces her nephew's developing difference as a misfortune. She is unaware that in this moment she has become the culture she fears her nephew will regularly encounter. She is supporting the ideal of heterosexuality as the pinnacle of the sexual identity hierarchy, in wanting "the best" or "easiest" for her nephew.

If there is no hierarchy, then we can explore freely, liberated from the limited or exalted status attached to our experience. We needn't be so concerned or panicked about what we *really* are. There is no need to defend, insist on, protect from or declare to. Our love, desire and affection are fluid experiences spilling over wherever they are drawn. They are not controlled by thought, by an idea of who we think we are or who we would like to be, or the status that it might bring us.

It is complicated to have a fluid identity, to not be so set in who we think we are, especially when certain ways of being are collectively rewarded and others not. This is obviously true not just for exploring love and sexuality, but for every aspect of human nature. The promise of rank or position blinds us and limits our ability to be open to the seemingly unusual experiences inside us. Even without the issue of status, having a fluid identity presents us with great challenges; it means being open to the continual flux and unpredictability of nature. In other words, we are not only who we think we are, but we are also that which lies just outside of those borders, that which is unknown and continually shapes and transforms us.

For example, I remember working with a married woman with children who described herself as a fundamentalist Christian. She came to see me because she was terrified that she was a lesbian and this was against all of her values. She found herself attracted to one of her friends. She repeatedly dreamt about this friend and felt totally obsessed with her. She wanted me to determine if she was *really* a lesbian. She looked at me with pleading eyes, ready to hear the worst. Unable to fluidly and openly explore the seemingly strange feelings and dreams that she was having, she waited in terror for my verdict.

In contrast, I worked with a man some years ago who strongly identified himself as gay and had never had sex with a woman. In one of our sessions, he had a powerful fantasy of impregnating a woman. After his initial shock and embarrassment, he was able to explore this fantasy, allowing it to enrich and expand his identity without questioning or worrying about who he *really* was.

It is threatening for those of us in the mainstream to consider that we might not *really* be heterosexual. For the sexual minority community, there is an added danger to identify so flexibly or unpredictably. We then become open prey for attack by absolutist challenge; our experience is judged as unstable, insecure, a phase, not "real." This has forced the gay community into the position of insisting on labels, set definitions of sexual experience and identity. It has been the only way to validate experience in a culture that only understands clear-cut, unchanging and absolute statements. Furthermore, the need to identify must intensify when such a powerful threat of annihilation by the mainstream exists.

This outer struggle too often becomes a painful inner process. The individual involved in a same-sex relationship might also wonder if what s/he is experiencing is "only a phase." In these moments, we are not fully able to experience and be proud of the relationship we are in. We are outside of it, thinking about the meaning and consequences of our affections. In doing so, we subtly, or not so subtly, put down or minimize our feelings and relationships. We are caught in the claws of the sexual identity hierarchy, unconsciously fighting and suffering at the bottom or striving and longing to be on top.

The paradox is that every experience in life is a phase, meaning that it is not permanent and cannot be relied on as unchanging. However, in the moments when we are in those experiences, we diminish them if we feel that we should be experiencing something else, or that one day we might be. We cannot really love or give of ourselves fully when in the background we feel that our experience is somehow not real or valid.

This is why some people from the sexual minority community react by asserting that their sexuality is the best. "After you have tried it with a woman you will never go back to men." This is a defense against an entire world culture that consistently affirms heterosexuality as the peak relationship possibility and sexual experience. It is a form of nationalism, sexual nationalism; as one side asserts its superiority the other responds in kind.

For the absolutist or nationalist, making something real means permanence and certainty. Very little in our universe is permanent, but that doesn't make it less real or less valid. We are fluid and changing expressions of nature, although we often behave as if we were established, set entities. Identity is always being challenged and shaped, dissolved and recreated. Matters of the heart are as fluid and surprising as the changes and movements of a river. Nature's work has no name or identity; it is simply the flow of experience, and the expression of our love.

I wish someone could have told me that when I was twenty. I still long for a culture that embraces the mystery of nature as its guide. And I honor Olga, the woman from Germany who dared to question who she really was. I will always remember her, and all of us who wonder who we *really* are, because that struggle belongs to us all.

Engraved in Stone: The Mythical Nature of the Teacher-Student Relationship

1917 Revisited

I saw my grave. I was walking down the most beautiful lonely beach when I saw a stone jutting out of the sand up ahead. I quickened my pace and trembled in disbelief, staring at the large block letters—my name was carved on that stone. The year of death was 1917. I awoke with a shock.

I explored this dream and had the distinct sense that this woman was a part of me, perhaps from another lifetime. Obviously she was a part of my spirit, since I dreamt about her. Who was this woman with my name who died long before I was born?

I imagined her as an ordinary woman of European descent who lived in a small town on the East coast of the United States. I saw clearly who I had been as that woman, her long white hair piled on top of her head, her blue dress with white trim meeting the short rubber boots just above her ankles. Her husband had died some years back and her children were busy with their own families. She had always been lonely.

A deep longing inside gave her no peace. Even in the happiest of moments, she was never really satisfied. Something always wanted more, looked further, peeked out from behind closed windows, looking beyond her family life and the town she lived in, beyond the borders of the so-called new world, into the skies, searching for the star that would answer her call.

As she lay taking her last breaths she promised herself she would never again return alone. In those short moments her whole life flashed before her and she was ready to leave it. As her spirit slowly escaped from her human form she saw the great teachings and teachers that would coax her into life the next time around.

Early Teachers

I wasn't the smartest kid in class and I wasn't a brownnoser, but many teachers seemed to like me. During the graduation ceremony at Preston Junior High School, I received a strange honor, the teacher's award. I am still not quite sure what that award really meant, except that a lot of teachers seemed happy with me. I do remember that I got $25 and felt simultaneously thrilled and embarrassed.

Junior high was not an easy time for me. The innocence of grammar school lifted, revealing ethnic and religious differences that we kids had never noticed before. Suddenly I had no friends and was fighting in daily battles against vicious anti-Semitic attacks in a predominantly Italian Catholic town. At a time when most kids are feeling the weight of peer pressure and worrying about fitting in, there was nothing I could do to fit in. As a result, I felt free to stand up for my own beliefs and interests. Already rejected, there was nothing for me to lose.

From time to time I was scared about the violence directed at me, which finally came to a head one day in the fall of eighth grade. A group of fifteen girls waited for me after school, along with a group of boys excited to watch the action. I stood at the top of the school steps wondering how I was going to make it the 100 feet to the school bus. My father's voice rang out in my ear. "If anyone hits you, make sure you hit them back." I held my breath and took the first steps towards the throng taunting me. When I reached the bottom of the stairs a few girls were immediately in my face, jeering and breathing on me. Maria pushed me with her books and suddenly the crowd surrounding me cleared as Gina Tonelli, the leader of the gang, made her way towards me. She got her hands on me and I balled my right hand into a fist and struck her right cheek. She fell to the ground, her girls surrounded her, and I tore onto the school bus. From then on no one messed with me, although I still remained friendless.

At a time when "cool" meant showing no interest in academics, dropping out of chorus and drama clubs, and seeing sports for girls as immature, I was left more or less to myself to pursue my interests. They certainly weren't cool, but I saw no reason to stop singing, shooting hoops, or studying, especially if dropping activities wasn't going to gain me friends. As a young girl circumstances had made me into an independent thinker, unafraid to stand for what I believed in. I think this is why teachers liked me. I spoke out in classes, asking questions and enjoying dialogue. Studying the Civil War engaged me emotionally and I spent hours creating a diary from the life of a slave. I bound a book of paper, ironing the sheets and burning the edges with matches, so it would look dated. I still remember that on the last page of the diary, my hero planned to kill himself rather than living a life in chains. Social issues moved me. Through my own experience of being an outsider, something beyond the ordinary life of being a young teen compelled me. I needed to find meaning in my life.

My high school was larger, a little more diverse, and again I sought out teachers who would inspire me. Teachers who stayed within the boundaries of the curriculum never ignited me. I was drawn to those individuals who were on the edge, the ones who supported my questions and challenges and joined me in defying the status quo. Swept up by some of the liberal changes of the early 1970s, some of my high school teachers invited us to call them by their first names, spoke openly about sexuality, and engaged in discussion around the social issues of our times.

Moving Out

Finally released from the confining town I grew up in, I welcomed the opportunity to study at a radical liberal arts college in the Midwest, where I met one of my most unexpected teachers. The education class was in a modern rectangular classroom with gray wall-to-wall carpet and no windows. I strolled in and did not know where to place myself in this large room with no chairs or tables. The room began to fill up as students of all different ages, even townspeople, scrambled to find a wall to lean against. As I scanned the sea of unknown faces, I wondered which one was the teacher.

To my utter surprise a voice from the floor began to quietly read aloud from the works of Carlos Castaneda. The chatter died down and I traced the serious tone to an indistinguishable white man in his fifties, with short gray hair, pressed slacks, and a light shirt with a jacket that looked like something my grandfather would wear. At a time when most of my teachers were wearing blue jeans, Ben Thompson was truly an anomaly.

Ben's appearance was so conservative and his demeanor so calm and steady, it was a shock to discover that he was actually the most provocative teacher on campus. I often wondered who he really was and at times was convinced he intentionally dressed so conventionally to make us question our perceptions of reality. I likened him to don Juan in Carlos Castaneda's writings, the unpredictable Yaqui shaman who always kept poor Carlos guessing.

Each semester Ben taught two classes. One was a required class for education majors entitled "Learner and the Learning Process." The second was a class devoted to the teachings of don Juan, based on the writings of Castaneda. I learned more about psychology and myself from these two classes than anything offered in the psychology department. Ben was interested in the big educational picture, the deeper process of learning, of personal development; his classes were a mix of psychology, philosophy, religion, shamanism, bodywork, sexuality and contemporary cultural studies. Confrontative and challenging, and awesomely terrifying, Ben taught us most strongly through personal example and interaction.

Although the same course titles appeared year after year in each semester offering, no course of Ben's ever repeated itself. I thrived in this spontaneous learning environment and loved his unpredictable teaching style. After officially enrolling in his classes my first semester, I made it a point throughout my college studies to attend his classes every semester. He took a liking to me and I blossomed in his presence.

A Growing Path

By the time I was in college, I was beginning to realize how crucial my teachers were. I needed guides, people to show me new paths to myself and the world. Life was too lonely and one-dimensional otherwise. I couldn't do it alone, couldn't touch the glowing life spirit beneath the weight of what felt like centuries of depression, nor could I fit in neatly to the conventional lifestyle of career and family that was expected of me. Something longed for the awesome, to touch the eternal mystery of life, to stretch myself beyond that which I knew. I had discovered these possibilities in part through the loving mentorship of my teachers.

I was in my third year of college when I met Arnold Mindell. Ben Thompson frequently spoke of this brilliant and unconventional man who was a Jungian analyst in Zurich, Switzerland. Ben shared his personal correspondence with us and read portions of Arny's early unpublished writings. I was enchanted and wondered about this man who had such profound insight and seemed to address a deep yearning inside of me.

Ben's love and admiration for Arny really touched me. One day as he read aloud from Arny's manuscript, Ben sighed loudly and had to pause. He shook his head in wonder, "I can't believe he is only thirty-eight, I think of him as sixty-five." I was moved by the genuine praise that an older man was able to give to a much younger one. When I finally met Arny I was surprised to learn that he had only met Ben in person once or twice. They must have had a profound effect on one another, because it seemed that they had known each other for years.

I planned an independent study course in Jungian psychology and traveled with my boyfriend for a few months of study with Dr. Arnold Mindell. At that time process-oriented psychology, or process work, did not formally exist by name. Arny was a Jungian analyst with a background in physics who was bringing together bodywork and Jungian psychology. A small circle of students had formed around him, and he offered informal classes.

I loved Arny before I even met him. Somehow I felt I had always known him. I don't know if it was because I had heard so much about him, or because I shared something with him that couldn't be contained by space and time. Nevertheless, the first time I walked into his modest office overlooking the lake of Zurich, I felt that I was coming home. I had spent my high school years isolated, searching for meaning in my life, and in college had tried a variety of bodywork, meditation, and other assorted personal development approaches. They all left me feeling like a failure. I never seemed to achieve the ideal body, movement, state-of-mind, or enlightened experience that was the goal of the given approach. At my first meeting with Arny I laid down my negative self-image before him. Filled with a potpourri of ideals and 70s new age sincerity, I conscientiously stated all of my shortcomings and conceptions about what I thought a "healthy," "normal" woman should be. Arny listened, and curiously inquired about my thinking. "Why was being loose better than being tight?" "Why should women be soft?" "Why should I be open and flexible?" He then interacted with me in a way that no one previously had. Instead of trying to change me, he was interested in exploring the experiences I was having. My tight, closed, angular experiences became passionate expressions, a movement dance that was fiery and emotional, spontaneous and direct. Here was my essence; dug up from the bowels of my being, outside the norms of so-called psychological health, and beyond the cultural views of gender roles. Arny joined me in this ecstatic state, jumping around his office, growling and shrieking, both of us letting our limbs flail out wherever they might go. After years of all of that pent-up energy, trying to contain all my enthusiasm and passion, trying to fit myself into a box of "normality"—finally I was free! At that moment I knew that this was just the beginning of a life-transforming relationship. Arny's unique ability to question the foundations of cultural beliefs and perceptions of reality would continually inspire me and resonate with a spirit deep inside of me.

Naïve about the etiquette of therapy, I let my feelings for him structure our relationship. I remember during one of my early sessions with him, his next client was late. I blurted out, "How lucky for me, I get to stay with you longer!" He seemed genuinely happy to have the time with me. His client never showed and I beamed in his presence. I never saw Arny as my therapist, a term which seemed limiting for the relationship I was developing with him. It sounded like problems, stuffy offices and rules that regulated the spirit between us. The term "therapist" didn't reflect the mysterious power that brought me to Zurich and inspired my life learning. I cherished the weekly hours I had with him, and by the time my studies were over, I knew that I would return to Zurich after graduating. I felt deeply called by the spirit of Arny and his teachings and knew I had to follow the yearning of my heart.

The Call of a Teacher

Carlos Castaneda was an anthropology student interested in studying the special powers of medicinal plants when he and a friend met the Yaqui Indian don Juan Matus at a bus station.[1] In this brief and seemingly insignificant encounter, Carlos found himself deeply affected by the old Indian from Sonora, Mexico. Don Juan told Carlos that he was at his service and that Carlos could visit him in Sonora. Carlos' friend dismissed don Juan as a crazy old man, but don Juan's shining eyes haunted Carlos, beckoning him in the months that followed until he ended up at don Juan's door. Don Juan seemed to appear as if he were waiting for Carlos, expecting his arrival.

Don Juan would say that power creates relationship, that a mysterious force brings people together for a deeper purpose. It was this power that so deeply affected Carlos, drawing him hundreds of miles to a man he did not know. This same power must have influenced don Juan to offer his services to a young American college student. Within their earliest meetings, their purpose together became more apparent.

Don Juan was baffled that the universe had indicated that Carlos was to be his apprentice, the recipient of his ancient teachings into the mysteries of becoming a "man of knowledge."[2] Carlos rapidly realized that he had met an awesome individual, a teacher who was to train him in the ancient shamanism and sorcery preserved by a remarkable band of individuals. During his challenging twenty-year relationship with don Juan, Carlos was often afraid, frustrated and on the verge of leaving permanently. However, he couldn't stay away; Carlos always returned, gripped by the learning that he experienced through his apprenticeship with don Juan.

In don Juan's view of the world, relationships are not created by will or intention, but by a far more mysterious power that brings people together. This greater power or spirit had called the two men and this call had to be honored. Travelling back to Zurich in the fall of 1980, I, too, was honoring a call that I could only follow without entirely knowing what it would bring me.

Love and Relationship

As my relationship with Arny began to develop, I became fascinated by the mythical aspects of the student-teacher relationship and began to learn more about this ancient and unique bond. The Castaneda books were a wonderful source of inspiration; don Juan's perspective gave me a view of relationships that are structured by a greater purpose. Many traditions view the relationship between teacher and student as sacred. Religious traditions elevate the relationship between the holy or spiritually enlightened leader and the members of his or her congregation. The ancient Greeks and Romans valued this special relationship; students would travel miles to dedicate themselves to the learnings of a particular teacher or philosopher. In India, especially in the tradition of Siddha Yoga, the guru is glorified as a divine being; through love and worship of the guru, the student discovers her own divine nature.[3]

Ben Thompson once told a story that has stuck with me all these years. A rich man brought his son to Socrates. "Please teach my son," said the father. Socrates looked at the boy and replied, "I'm sorry I can't." "I will give you much money," the father pleaded. "It is not possible. Your son doesn't love me."

Socrates, like many great teachers, understood that love is central for great learning and teaching. I learned early on that without love, learning is dry and lacks spirit or inspiration. Love has spurred me on, inspired me to reach further than I knew was possible. During times in my life when I have felt unable to go on, when I have been riddled with self-doubt and inner criticism, a teacher's love and belief in me has given me new direction, breathed new life into a tortured soul. It could not have been anyone's love that would have had that effect on me. For me, the experience of a teacher's love is unique. I can remember many days over the last twenty years of my life, lying on the floor in Arny's office, feeling that somehow my life had no meaning: my relationships were troubled or severed; I felt without purpose or creativity, or I felt I had no place or value in the world. In just minutes in his presence my world changed. Suddenly I was filled with love, felt connected to my purpose, to the divine spark inside myself. What was happening? How could my inner state of mind have changed so dramatically? The power of love inspires great inner change. This is not just a love that assures or comforts, but a love that brings us into contact with parts of ourselves that we didn't know existed, that penetrates to the awesome core of the spirit taking us out of our ordinary state of perception. Don Juan referred to this perceptual change as a shifting of the assemblage point. In Indian culture the term *shakti pat* describes the divine love that is transferred from the guru and transforms everyday consciousness.

Taking someone as a teacher comes from dreams and deep yearnings and acknowledges a kindred spirit endowed with great wisdom and guidance that is elevated beyond an ordinary view of reality. Of course this teacher is us; the teacher represents a wise or divine aspect of ourselves that we long to get close to. Embodying our deepest potential, the teacher inspires us through love and relationship, which brings us closer to this inner divinity. Loving a teacher can also offer a chance to trust in something greater than ourselves, a divine submission to which we can yield because we know we submit to the deepest parts of ourselves. In the darkest times love's light reminds us of our eternal natures. Learning through the loving and love of a teacher can help us feel deeply connected to everything.

Power, Abuse and Relationship

In modern Western society it is controversial to talk about the adoration of a teacher. Due to the overwhelming abuse of power, such feelings between student and teacher are not only a sensitive subject, but are often taboo. As a result of the taboos and very real dangers around close student/teacher relationships in American culture, mentoring relationships in educational institutions, spiritual domains, or in social services are regulated by laws.

Human experience becomes taboo and highly regulated when we are at a loss to go further in our interactions with one another. I have met many people who speak with great fondness toward teachers or authority figures; however, I have heard numerous stories in my practice about teachers who were brutal and cruel, and left the scars of shame and humiliation. This experience of public abuse carries over in our lives, making us afraid to speak up, afraid to question or criticize authority, or to bring in our own individual style. Teachers have great powers, and if they lose awareness of their power, it results in the abuse that many of us have suffered.

Power used unconsciously keeps us from feeling free to conflict. We feel we must adapt to the authority and hold back essential aspects of our personality. To conflict openly might be punished; we might fall out of favor, lose our position, or lose love. In those moments we might resort to lying and harbor secrets, fearing repercussions if we were truthful. We might give up aspects of our lives or discard relationships that the authority might object to. Finally, we might engage in a more intimate relationship with an authority than feels comfortable, unaware that we acted under duress and force. This is a moment when the culture peeks in, fears coercion and calls foul play. The relationship is now handled by lawyers and other authorities.

Teachers, therapists, religious leaders and other authorities use power unconsciously when we interact with someone and we are not aware of our social or psychological advantages.[4] At these times, we don't see that we feel at ease in the interaction, but the other appears uncomfortable and usually cannot even voice this. In contrast, when we are aware of these power differences, we notice how other people feel around us and we address this atmosphere. We use our power to bring up the discomfort and call attention to how our own behavior might contribute to the discomfort of the other. We examine ourselves to discover how we might inadvertently inhibit or intimidate others. We might ask if there is something we could do that could make the other more comfortable. We encourage individuals to differ and bring in their own opinions, to conflict and criticize without consequence. We feel free to step outside of our role as a teacher or authority and make all aspects of ourselves available.

A teacher who is aware of her powers can offer her student a great gift. Learning how to differ and conflict, how to interact with those who have more power and to express the fullness of one's personality, is incredibly important. Disagreeing with an authority provides a chance to work through past abuse and trauma when we felt limited in our expression, and were too young or powerless to disagree. We can discover courage and inner strength and new patterns of interacting with someone who has more power. At the same time our love and relationship to our teacher expands as we experience new parts of ourselves. Although cultural regulations are important, they can also create artificial relationships, keep emotional distance between people, and can prevent us from connecting to inner powers as we learn how to differ and conflict with those in authority.

The Courage to Conflict

Since I came of age in the early 1970s, conflicting with authority was part of my daily bread. However, conflicting against a system presents little personal risk compared to disagreeing interpersonally with someone you respect who is in a position of power. Differing with a boss, therapist, doctor, teacher, religious leader, even a friend or family member, can be a great challenge. At these moments many of us become hopeless and withdraw in relationship, disagreeing by retreating and maybe by gossiping about the person later.

Arny encouraged my own thinking, even when it went against his. He picked up my discomfort with him, noticed criticisms and doubts that I was terrified to voice. He warmly urged me to engage with him, telling me that he had many flaws and could surely learn from my perceptions. I was shocked, thrilled, and terrified all at once. No one had ever encouraged my criticisms with the certainty that our relationship would improve. As a great teacher, Arny saw that part of my development was to feel free with him, not only to love him, but to disagree and conflict and assert my own personality.

Transference and Countertransference

These days, many people satisfy their longing for a teacher by seeing a therapist. Psychotherapy knows about the intense love that can occur between the client and therapist and structures it into the therapeutic process. Transference is a term used to describe the client's feelings towards the therapist, meaning that the client has projected strong feelings and aspects of his process onto the therapist. Countertransference is a term used to describe the therapist's projected feelings in regard to the client.

The feelings of both client and therapist are assumed to be intra-psychic processes with no outer relationship value. In this type of therapeutic framework the therapist does not engage relationally with either transference or countertransference experiences. Working with the powerful feeling experiences of the transference the client can learn a great deal about her own projected inner powers. This is important work and is particularly useful for those people who are looking for a therapist who will reflect their process back to them, without personal exchange. However, it does not address those who learn within the context of relationship.

Fitting human feeling into a therapeutic concept can neglect the living experience of human relationship. Concepts that rigidify and codify our feeling life limit experience. The mysterious and spiritual connection that don Juan alludes to is not included in this view of relationships. In most therapeutic approaches, relationship does not really exist—only "therapeutic relationship," which means that all relationship interactions reflect the client's psychology. The feelings that the client has towards the therapist are only valid for the psychological growth of the client and are not validated within the relationship itself. If we cannot have an impact in our relationships, over time we feel ineffectual, which can reinforce the feeling of powerlessness.

The idea of resistance is a prime example. Many schools of psychology claim that when the client does not go along with the therapist's line of thinking, they are resisting. The client is seen to be fighting off his parents or other authority figures or defensive in opening up to a part of himself that the therapist sees. The difference of perception that client and therapist are having is not seen as a conflict asking to be addressed in the relationship, but as an inner process that the client must work through. Both of these viewpoints are valid, often simultaneously. The client needs to differentiate his feelings towards authority figures and resist the inner parts of himself that are putting him down. Additionally, the therapist might be unaware of her power and how she is putting the client down. To only work on this process intrapsychically, without valuing the outer experience that the client has in relationship to the therapist, reinforces the impotence that the client feels towards authority figures by invalidating the client's perceptions in relationship. By engaging directly in relationship with the client, the therapist offers the client a chance to experience and grow from a real interaction. To do this, the therapist must be aware of her own authority and powers and be open to looking at her own perceptual holes. The therapist then models an authority who is open to learning while also encouraging the client to directly conflict with her.

For example, one of my first clients in Switzerland was a German woman who was married to a very successful Swiss man twenty years her senior. Her father was very authoritative and often cruel. For most of the year that I worked with her, she "resisted" everything I suggested. We worked with her resistance intrapsychically, seeing that she was in a fight with her father and often felt inferior to her husband. Through her resistance she was attempting to feel her own strength and gain power relative to her husband and inner father. This was helpful; however, the resistance in our work persisted until I engaged in relationship with her.

Finally, I told her that I felt powerless and unable to help her. She smiled as if she had won a great battle. I told her that I felt that I wasn't up to her. She held her head up and puffed her chest out. Seeing these subtle body signals, I suggested that she didn't need me anymore and that she seemed confident and able to go into the world and stand for what she believed in. I told her that I believed in her independence and that if she were to need me I would be available. She breathed a sigh of relief and said that was exactly what she needed.

When I engaged in relationship with her, she was able to have a genuine experience of her power relative to me, someone in an authority position. It took me some development to be able to do this with her. Due to my own insecurities about my beginning work as a therapist, I didn't really want to see that she had grown out of me. I didn't want to lose a client; therefore, it was to my benefit to only work with her issues of authority and resistance outside of the relationship to me. I was holding onto my power and position because I didn't want to lose her.

In fear of potential abuse and damaging power differences, therapy has sanitized relationships. However, therapists who do not work in relationship with their clients could be inadvertently abusive. The therapist who unconsciously uses her power by insisting on her perceptions while disregarding the negative feedback of her client is misusing her psychological power.

Divine Transference

Transference can be a deep experience and an incredible growth opportunity. My feelings for Arny were instantaneous and have deepened since our first meeting in 1979. One of my earliest dreams about him was that we were exchanging rings. I felt we were eternally connected by a love beyond the boundaries of this lifetime. I see my relationship with him, as with other important teachers in my life, as an answered promise to the woman in my dream who died in 1917. She would not return unless she had the guidance of a beloved teacher to accompany and inspire her on her path. I understand that dream and experience as central to who I am.

Writing about love, in particular the intense love of a teacher, is not common in my culture. To many readers, my sentiments will seem strange and perhaps blasphemous. It is an experience that is essential to my path in life, but certainly not for everyone. However, it does find a more resounding echo in other cultures.

In India, Siddha yoga is a spiritual practice of learning through the love of a teacher or guru. The disciple meditates constantly on the loving image of the guru until she can see her own divinity reflected in the guru's eyes. The search for enlightenment, divine experience and self-development is highly valued in India and other Asian cultures and in most cases the relationship to a teacher is seen as crucial to this process.

Many westerners who have similar longings but no formal path of study or cultural pattern for such learning travel to other cultures searching for guides. Western psychology acknowledges this drive in aspects of the positive transference, when the client "projects" transpersonal or loving qualities onto the therapist.

Years back I was at a training seminar for process-oriented therapists. We gathered as therapists and students in order to learn more about working with one another, while Arny supervised our work. I was sitting in the circle when a woman who I had known for a few years asked if I would be her therapist. Nervous about public supervision but excited at the opportunity, I jumped in.

Many years later I cannot recall the content of her presenting difficulty. However, I do remember her face beaming and mine blushing. She really liked me, she said, and felt she could learn something from me. I was shy to notice her adoration and I didn't know what to do with the love and admiration that was coming my way. Arny intervened and asked me if I was noticing her admiration. I think my face must have turned from a shy pink to a bright red. Arny noticed that I was hesitant to accept her love and to help her discover and deepen it. He asked her what she saw in me. As I squirmed, she told me that she saw a goddess.

This was a deep learning experience for me. Arny helped me to open up and allow her to see my divine nature by encouraging her perceptions of me. Then he guided me to help her see those same divine qualities in herself. We were both working at the borders of our known world, stretching our identities to go beyond ourselves as ordinary women. Glowing, two goddesses sat in mutual admiration, connected with the deepest strata of their beings.

This was one of my earliest experiences working therapeutically with someone with this kind of divine transference. I obviously had been in the position of adoring, but not so powerfully the object of it. Therapists rarely talk about the gifts of such transference experiences. I guess we are shy or think the experiences that our clients have of us have nothing to do with us—they are just transferred. I do not think this is the only truth. Clients do see our divine natures and need us to accept their love and perception. In addition, they want a connection with this sacred part of themselves.

A therapist or teacher who cannot accept such love denies an essential part of their own humanity and inhibits the feelings of their client or student. It is painful to love someone and not be received. Due to the therapist's limits, the client learns to express love sparingly and to not let the full effects of being loved inside.

In the past, I had often felt Arny's slight discomfort when I expressed my love towards him. He accepted it, but I also had the sense he wanted to get away from it. One day we were sitting with a group of people at a seminar, and I was feeling so grateful for all that I had received and learned from him over the years. My heart was full of immense love and eternal gratitude. As I expressed some of my feelings, his eyes began to shine and he held my gaze for what seemed forever. I felt my love was totally received. He then thanked me for loving him so much. It was a great gift to be loved by me, he said. I felt elated to be so deeply received and to love so freely.

Arny then told us that he had made a leap in his own personal growth. He too had been shy to accept the love and adoration coming his way. He had recently been in India, where an Indian man told Arny that he was his guru. Arny told him that he wasn't a guru, he didn't want to be worshipped and that the man should find someone else to worship. The man insisted, saying that Arny was his guru even if Arny didn't accept it. Arny then realized that these sacred longings were stronger than any one person's will and that it was an inflation to not accept them. He then accepted this man's feelings and thanked him for being his teacher. At first glance, it seems inflated and arrogant, or even blasphemous to be worshipped, to accept being seen as a god. However, if we reject a spiritual yearning by not heeding the call, we are putting ourselves above divine will and rejecting a numinous love that is meant to be experienced. The actual inflation is to go against this greater will.

Projection or Relationship?

As a therapist steeped in the psychotherapeutic process, I have thought about the transference and its seemingly logical conclusion that the strong feelings the client has about the therapist are projections that must be eventually integrated by the client. I often thought about this in my own relationship with Arny.

At one point I became troubled, telling myself that I should be able to reown those qualities that I saw in Arny. My quandary was not that I couldn't. I could access him inside of me, see him as a part of me. However, I didn't want to! This was a shock to me. I didn't want to just take my experience internally, because I felt that only seeing my feeling as a projection cut off a huge part of me. I wanted to love. I enjoyed loving Arny and being loved by him.

I then asked Arny how he had dealt with this duality in his life. I knew he had had a therapist whom he loved very much who had died. I told Arny that I didn't want to integrate him or take back my projections. I enjoyed loving him. He smiled, looking like he understood me. He said that both views are important and are not meant to exclude each other. It is essential to see that what you perceive in your teacher is you. Simultaneously, the feelings you have toward your teacher in relationship are real and are meant to be lived out and experienced. I felt greatly relieved.

This duality does not just exist in mentoring relationships, but in all relationships. We are drawn to people who mirror parts of ourselves, especially parts of ourselves that we have less awareness of and need to develop. We can ask ourselves: is this really relationship? Is it just narcissism? Am I just relating to that person for my own personal growth? The answer is both yes and no. All relationships inspire us in our personal development and elicit interactions and experiences that we can grow from. But this is not a pathological tendency; the experience of relating is just as important as the personal growth that transpires.

This brings up basic existential questions. Does relationship exist without projection? What is relationship, really? Besides being a vehicle for all of us to develop, relationship also offers companionship and community. If we take our drive to relate seriously and notice our often unconscious tendencies to project, we might realize that we are everyone and are deeply related. Sometimes we don't project enough; we too easily split off other people's realities from our own. For example, we admire a friend's intelligence and neglect to discover that this brilliance is also a part of us. Or we gossip about how arrogant another person is, neglecting that we also feel superior at times. On a world level we might ignore the suffering and experiences of others, thinking that we are separate. In these situations we need to project more, go more deeply into our experiences and fantasies to see that we really are them. From the viewpoint of relationship, the better our connection with someone, the more inspired we feel to develop personally.

Sacred Roots

It is uncomfortable for some people to read about gurus and teachers and the love and adoration that some of us feel. I think this discomfort is caused in part by our lack of contact with our own divinity. We do not value it. Although many religions emphasize our divine nature, it is not the message most of us seem to pick up. Judeo-Christian religion states that man has been created in the image of God, meaning that we are all holy beings. Catholicisim teaches that the holy spirit resides in each of us. The goal of Buddhism is to discover one's buddha nature, the Buddha within. The pantheon of Taoist gods and goddesses reside in the body. The Hindu god and goddess Shiva and Shakti are body experiences waiting to happen. In many tribal and indigenous cultures, spirits and ancestors speak through individuals.

Although these ancient beliefs lend us support, it is challenging to see the divine nature in people. We are often one-sidedly materialistic and rational and lose contact with the mystery of life and the numinous experience of loving.

From this viewpoint, the mentoring relationship can be a great vessel to develop and experience the deep spiritual longings of our beings. The transference in psychology really is about transferring, but is too often understood only in terms of the client's process. However, a great gift is transferred from client to therapist and then from therapist to client. Back and forth flow the love and adoration, a mutual outpouring of devotion and respect. It belongs to no one and everyone. It is like the sun we all share. When someone shines their loving sunshine in our direction, we feel connected to the divine roots of creation.

Independence and Freedom

Many of us also become uncomfortable around loving a teacher because we fear we will lose our own free will. Particularly in the United States, freedom is often associated with independence. We value the self-made individual and see dependency as a sign of weakness. We are often afraid to love or become emotionally attached for fear we will need others and lose our independence. However, if we must keep ourselves in check, fearing that we might be overwhelmed or swept away by love and emotion, we are not independent. We are imprisoned, unfree to have the experiences that are inside of us.

A certain kind of humility might be missing when we pride ourselves on being self-made or independent. We are asserting that we are all-powerful and don't see the spiritual forces, relationships, and dreams that are out of our control and have helped and guided us on our paths. When freedom is associated only with independence, we might miss the awesome and liberating experience of submission. In my own experience, submitting to something greater than myself, or entrusting myself to the love and guidance of another human being, is a powerful experience, one that I have also experienced as paradoxically liberating. For many of us it is when we have been beaten down, depressed and at the very bottom, or near death, when nature and circumstance force a painful submission that amazing transformations occur. At these moments we do not know who we are anymore; we have given up everything that we have known and this makes room for something else to appear.

I was once in Italy in the small village of Assisi, the birthplace of Saint Francis. I met a man in a restaurant who told me about his transformation. He said he used to gamble and drink a lot, and was abusive to his wife and family. Then he had a car accident and almost died. As he was coming to consciousness he saw the gentle face of St. Francis. At that moment, he realized that love was essential, that something more powerful was leading his life, and that he had to make big changes. I tell this story not because it is unusual, but because it is so common.

Whenever we drop our idea of who we think we are, we expand our identity and submit to something greater. Taoism urges us to follow the Tao, to drop all of our preconceived notions and align ourselves with the sacred pulse of nature. Some of the martial arts, particularly Aikido, are based on the concept of yielding to nature. In the United States we rarely witness sacred aspects of submission. We are taught not to give in or give up, to stand firm in our beliefs. To yield is perceived as losing. No wonder loving a teacher can make us feel so guarded and insecure.

Love can be seen as a great transformer. It can melt the most rigid of identities. One of the reasons falling in love is such an awesome experience is because we yield to something greater than ourselves. At these times in life we experience new aspects of ourselves. Our routines might be disrupted, we might experience the world and others differently, and we might find ourselves open to new experiences in ways that we previously couldn't imagine.

Mythical Callings

The woman bearing my name who died in 1917 has had a great influence on me. I can understand and appreciate my great need for teachers and relationship. I would not suffer the loneliness and isolation of living life without the inspirational relationships that help me to grow beyond myself and the pervasive dominance of conventional reality. This is a reason to be born, to live; it is an eternal exploration that seems to take me beyond the boundaries of my life.

Some people connect with divine and sacred experience through their love of God, Christ, Buddha, Shakti, Allah or the Tao. Still others connect with these transpersonal experiences in nature or through meditation or in altered states of consciousness. Some people reach ecstatic states by dancing, singing, painting, inventing or writing. Many of us have these experiences with a lover and in sexual contact. And some of us will discover our divine centers through the love and adoration of a teacher.

End Notes

[1] See Carlos Casteneda, *The Teachings of Don Juan* (Berkeley: University of California Press, 1968); *A Separate Reality* (NY: Simon and Schuster, 1971), *Journey to Ixtlan* (NY: Simon and Schuster, 1972); *Tales of Power* (NY: Simon and Schuster, 1974).

[2] Casteneda, *Teachings*.

[3] Swami Muktananda, *The Play of Consciousness* (Camp Meeker, CA.: SYDA Foundation, 1974).

[4] See Arnold Mindell, *Sitting in the Fire* (Portland, OR: Lao Tse Press, 1995), for a complete discussion on power, rank and privilege.

Mother and Child

I.
It Takes a Baby to Raise a Village

You were still spirit when I took you in my arms and held your wriggling body up to the heavens. "Welcome," I said. "Welcome to this world. We are so glad you are here. We love you so much." You looked directly at me with shining eyes and said confidently, "I know."

Still wet from the other world, you arrived knowing you were loved and belonged. You were full of yourself as all newborns are; full and still close to the source of eternal nourishment. We were delighted to welcome you, to give you the care and love that earthly parents can; but you held greater powers and we could see them. Still at one with the mystery of your heartbeat, you knew the source that breathed your first independent breaths, the origins of creation that sustain each of us regardless of circumstance. Birthed from the dreamy, murky waters of creation, fed by spirit and formed by mystery, we are all first loved, the message indelibly printed in our cells.

Your presence works as a love charm. Pure of spirit and intent, uncorrupted by self-doubt and ambition, the cord to heaven, still intact, tugs on the longing of others. These irresistible forces pull on grown men and women. Our eyes become magnets tracking each gesture and movement. We reach for you, can't keep our hands off you. Lips brush against plump velvet skin and our noses stick to you, inhaling your essence. No edge to intimacy, no fear to come too close, your flesh is ours.

Babies are public goods. It takes a baby to raise a village. Who else can bring together the incompatible, infect us with a dizzying love and draw out the elder of the earth? Perhaps the young are meant to do this, to teach us about love and to parent what has been neglected.

In my local coffee shop I notice an elderly couple. A man and a woman sit despondently and stir their coffee. The woman glances to her left and in a flash her eyes regain their luster. I follow her line of vision and discover a young man holding a puppy only a few weeks old. The woman has lost all interest in her coffee; she is transfixed by the younger man holding this adorable creature to his chest. Full of parental pride, he can sense her eyes pulling on the bundle in his arms. He gravitates to her table and she can hardly contain the sudden rush of joy that pulses through her veins. Her smile is as wide as the gulf that had lain between them. Just as she is about to ask, the younger man offers, "Would you like to hold him?" Her eyes mist over and she can hardly answer as her arms reach out instinctively to receive the gift of new birth. The puppy nestles himself between her breasts and she holds him close and coos, losing herself in the joy of her own loving. Her husband looks on equally transformed, waiting his turn to hold precious young life.

II.
The Birth of the Mother

Another year goes by. I am worried. A longing that loses itself in words gnaws at my hind-brain. Is it culture, biology, the great spirit, or my own mothering nature? Who calls the children into this world? How do they really get here? How does the spirit find the womb, the vehicle of transition? How does woman know when her womb is sought?

Torn with doubt and longing, I wonder, "When is the mother born?" At the tail end of my childbearing years, I still feel like a child; I seek care and assurance, long for elders to acknowledge my existence. I treasure my freedom, fear new regimens that limit spontaneity. I catch a glance of my naked body in the mirror, look again. How could this body carry a child? I look down at my flat stomach, wondering how life will stretch and mold me. I like my athleticism and ease in movement, and imagine the aftereffects of a body ravaged by motherhood.

In the quiet of the night Mother is calling. I hear the echoing cries of ancestors luring me to take my place. "It is time," they whisper. "I feel too young, not ready, too much a child myself," I counter. Too much longing for the parent I never had, a child raised by children looking for parents. Not that my parents were any different than most others; the world is full of children raising children. So many people, so few elders.

Mother is sneaking into my bones without my knowing it. I feel the kindness in my eyes, the relaxation of Mother's gaze. I breathe easily, settling into myself. I surrender to the call of the ancestors, let it penetrate. Piercing through callused skin needed to defend, mother love does its magic. Sinking into the body, following these earthly rhythms, she is present. Ancient wisdom leads me and mother stands by with her blessing.

The child in me panics. "How can I carry this child? How can my hips widen to hold so much, carry the burden of life, all of it?" A child-product of children striving for the ultimate and permanent goal of youth, I want my hips intact, narrow and sleek, my breasts firm and stomach taut. Where is the beauty in motherhood? I fear I will become a matron and join the mothers who seem formless and without sex. Hypnotically addicted to youth, the young soul sees no beauty in the organic development of the body, the inevitable maturation of life's years. Only young children are still old enough to be fascinated by the folds of aging skin, to feel and experience the varying textures of nature's creation, to curl up in the warm quiet wisdom of age.

I fear I will pass on the same oppressive expectations I barely endured; that I will judge my child as if the child were a reflection of me and wince at deviation, unable to embrace it. Often afraid to support my own individual path, I may consequently be unable to nourish the growing life now in my care. Mainstream norms act like a vice inside and outside me. I would need to have the detachment of a sage or a dying person to raise a child. Why don't the dead raise our children? They seem much more able—closer to the spirit of new birth, not attached to the clockwork of this world.

I didn't know I was hopeless. I remember that day in school. I was sixteen and the teacher asked the girls how many of us thought we wanted to have children. I was the only one who didn't raise my hand. I answered proudly that this is not the kind of world I would want to bring children into. Depressed, angry and marginalized, as a teenager I couldn't imagine propagating what I was experiencing around me. I felt outraged at the blind ease with which young women unquestioningly asserted their mark on motherhood. "These are the mothers," I thought in disbelief and fell more deeply into the throes of hopeless rage. Who are the mothers and fathers that have created the suffering around me, that make the future look so bleak? Who hears the cries of the world? Who is accountable? Where are the teachers of spirit? Where is the mother who is outside time and the limits of convention, able to penetrate into the most hopeless of times and reveal new life?

It is the birth of the mother that seems so formidable in this world of young souls. I dig into my flesh searching for the roots of mother-life. Tucked under ancient folds, secure between bone and muscle, the gestating seeds are sprouting. "Rejoice!" The songs of the ancestors vibrate inside me, relentlessly chanting, enticing me to take my place. I answer the call with calmness.

III.
Ode to Myself

I would have loved to have mothered myself, pulled my slippery form out from the birth canal and held nature's ineffable creation to my breast. I would coo and bask in the wonderment of new life as all new mothers do, transfixed by every gesture and sound.

It is so easy to mother the baby! I effortlessly take her into my arms and look deeply into those mud brown eyes, dark as a night sky shining with stars. She is irresistible. My love pours out and I fear drowning her in my rapture. I cannot love her enough. My heart feels like it will burst with the mother love that pulses through me. I am totally taken, swept off my feet in an ecstasy of complete focus and devotion. I welcome each part of her as new experiences tumble from her as often as she drools. Oh, to have been the mother of myself, to have been melted and opened by my first smile.

Who is it that perceives me now, watches me close with what I had hoped would be mother love? No one here to see the miraculous, to kiss my wounds and coo over my first steps. Instead I meet with conditions and cautions, going forward with great trepidation, no faith or belief in my being. I cannot remember the mother's perception that greeted me at birth, fascinated with the irrepressible expression of my bubbling life spirit. How she pulled me in so close assuring me that she would always be present, giving me the sense of eternal home.

This timeless mother saw me through my years (and watches over me now). She encouraged the wisdom in my young voice and guided me to the deepest murmurs in my heart. She taught me to follow the ways of nature and believed in my dreams. She was my ally in confronting injustice and knew how to heal the wounds of despair. When life's changes took their course she helped me to stand proud, not ashamed of my growing breasts and gangly limbs, welcoming the blood of my womanhood in joyous celebration. Mother made me feel beautiful and taught me how to love my feelings in a world hostile to them. Mother watered the child in her garden, kissed the newly forming buds with her sunshine and applauded the wild shoots that grew in all directions.

If I had known the baby it would have been easier to discover the mother. At the moment of birth mother cannot be contained; first cries claim her as a little mouth reaches for nourishment. Eyes turned inward, glued shut content in the dreaming world, struggle to open and find Mama. She is infected, deliriously captivated, called to take the role she cannot deny. But I wasn't there to witness the event of my birth, to be irrevocably moved to love and care for this new life.

I was not there. But Mother was. Mother carries us even when the people around us are not able to. No baby is ever born without Mother; she is always there—always has been, always will be. Each birth is complete; mother and child emerge together as a whole, each new life mothered implicitly. For who gives us the faith to breathe our first breaths? Who has supported our earliest impulses to cry and gurgle? Who has nurtured the spirit of life that runs through us and given us the uninhibited gift of self-expression? Mother is present, holding her new life form; with grace and strength her presence is the key to our freedom and self-love.

Healing History

History Class Revisited

"History repeats itself," my ninth grade history teacher told us. He dryly proclaimed that the world could learn from its mistakes if only we studied history. This might have been his attempt to scare us into studying more, but judging by the faces of the jaded youth around him, his point was not particularly inspiring.

I remember wrestling with the ramifications of his cool pronouncement. War, injustice, poverty, slavery, genocide, all destined to repeat themselves! What kind of a world was I coming of age in? How could he be so cool? If he had any passion or heat in his words, he might have awakened us, but he seemed so resigned. Was it hopelessness, superiority, acceptance? With that kind of an attitude, how could anything change?

In retrospect, I think his most honest statement might have been that he didn't have answers. Although he might have hoped that historical study would change the future, his delivery betrayed him. His monotone voice and cool demeanor gave little hope or heartening direction. He, like many of the adults I had encountered, did not know what to do. They could give advice and cite the history that repeated itself. "So, what then?" my heart cried out in despair. I wanted to pull them out of their chairs and into the heat of the world I was growing up into. I saw the repetition. I watched JFK, Dr. King, Robert Kennedy and Malcolm go down, and I watched hope go down with them. Was Richard Nixon the best we could do? The fire of my adolescence ignited. How could historical awareness calm the human heart and stop the cycles of power, abuse and revenge?

Standoffs

In a U.S. city a group of 200 people have gathered to work on diversity issues. The atmosphere tightens as the topic of racism comes to an emotional head. A white man feels threatened by the communication style of a black man. Instead of cowering in fear, he returns the threat, demanding that the black man change his approach. Tempers flare and both men scream in each other's faces. Suddenly a group of white people surrounds the white man and pleads with him to see the inherent racism in his demand that the black man adapt to a more "acceptable" communication style. The words have little impact as the white man becomes more provocative, insisting that he is free to say what he wants. The black man is joined by a group of supporters—this conflict couldn't get much hotter.

In another group setting in a European city the issue of anti-Semitism and German responsibility for World War II is on the table. On one side, Jewish people from all over the world express their pain and reveal family stories of the holocaust. There is little response from the other side. A German group has formed, standing and silent. "What do you feel?" a Jewish woman cries out in anguish. "I feel badly, but this was a long time ago and has nothing to do with our generation," a German man says. His comments inflame the group, voices rise, and the German wall stands more defiantly.

The white man in the first gathering was a high school teacher in a diverse district. Surely, he knew his history. Was he even aware of repeating the legacy he teaches about? The German participants in the second situation were of various ages and tired of living with the awareness of the holocaust. Both of these parties, steeped in education and the historical knowledge of their culture, were repeating the history they deplored.

These individuals were not white supremacists or neo-Nazis. How did they step into this landmine? History was repeating itself right in front of our eyes. In the first scene, the white master was setting the rules of the house and there would be consequences if the black man didn't comply. The modern-day white man can leave and feel justified in his beliefs because he can retreat to the comfort and security of the mainstream white world where his rules reign, rules that mirror his unconscious supremacist beliefs about how the world should be and how people should communicate. In the other scenario we could have been back in Hitler's Germany when the majority of German citizens stood silent and closed their eyes to the horror around them. Then and now, a marginalized group has cried out in pain and nobody hears.

The Inheritance

We inherit the legacy of our ancestors, not only the things we can see and lay our hands on, like technological conveniences, but the unresolved social and emotional issues of the day. Most white North Americans think that U.S. slavery was so long ago that it has nothing to do with them. Whites tend to think that they weren't responsible and that people should move on, that the playing field is level and there is no need for government attempts, such as affirmative action, to amend history. This mainstream votes for legislation that becomes tougher on drugs, creates more prisons, and cuts welfare without addressing the deeper issue of racism that has partially birthed these problems. In fact, the slavery of African Americans was not so long ago; there are still a handful of elderly people in this country whose parents were ex-slaves[1] and many more whose grandparents were born into slavery. All black people living today have first-hand experiences of racism. This seems obvious to many people, but must be emphasized again and again.

The horror of the holocaust is very alive for Jewish people, particularly Jewish survivors and their families. And yet, the Jewish community often meets indifference and loathing when this history comes forward. Americans and Europeans alike want to put it behind them. In the new Germany, Germans want to be free from the past. Since Jewish culture has become a distant memory throughout Europe, it has been easier to avoid. Jews in all countries throughout the world have experienced some form of anti-Semitic insult and discrimination.

How does the United States today deal with racism? The white community is embarrassed by it. They don't want to see how immediate and alive this racist heritage is. They want to put it behind them and have "normal" relationships with black people. They are not like their racist ancestors; they aren't racist. They have black co-workers, acquaintances, maybe friends. Many try to have relationships in the black community, and when they feel rebuked they don't understand why.

In 1997, over one hundred and thirty years late and due to significant pressure, then-President Clinton apologized to African Americans on behalf of the United States for the crime of slavery. A short conflict then ensued as to whether the government should appropriate reparations. Clinton's decision not to offer any form of restitution reflects mainstream opinion that present generations of black people are on equal economic footing. This view dismisses the racism that has supported the undue weight of poverty that blacks have carried.

Europeans and Germans deal with the history of the holocaust and anti-Semitism similarly to how white Americans deal with the legacy of slavery and the reality of racism. It is an embarrassment, another blemish on their history, a shameful time, but it has been surmounted. "There is no anti-Semitism now, only by neo-Nazis," a German woman tells me. Here lies the greatest danger. Neo-Nazi groups are seen as splinter groups, young fanatics that need to be stopped. What is not seen is subtle anti-Semitic behavior, how a neo-Nazi attitude exists in mainstream consciousness whenever we turn silent or look away, whenever we can't stand to see a Jewish person show her pain. This same dynamic occurs when we think that racism only exists in the extreme and flagrant acts of white supremacist groups, and we do not examine ourselves for the subtle racist thoughts and behaviors that are a part of our culture. Here lies the real threat of history repeating itself.

Does time heal? Time can dull the pain and allow future generations ignorance, but it does not heal. Time passes the baton to a generation a little more removed. The distance can give perspective and insight and can assist in making real emotional change, or people can use the distance to retreat, making conflict more intractable. When social issues become most intractable, we are in danger of history repeating. Matters of the heart do not vanish, but demand our attention. The more we disengage, the more violently these unresolved issues will manifest.

When Wars End

When war ends, our work has just begun. The joy of being reunited with loved ones and stopping the carnage and agonies of war consume us all. However, stopping the fight is only the most basic step in working on world or social issues. Relief momentarily satisfies us; the euphoria of the victors and devastation of the losers hypnotizes us. While everyone celebrates or mourns, the issues that escalated the conflict remain unaddressed. What happens after war is perhaps even more essential.

When the Second World War ended, the allied forces forced "naïve" local villagers into the concentration camps so they would see the horror that had existed in their neighborhoods. Many German people had claimed ignorance to the atrocities in their own backyards. Now that they knew, what were they going to do? At the Holocaust Museum in Washington D.C., I learned what many of these people did and did not do. After the war, many Jews tried to return to their hometowns in Germany, Poland, and other European countries that had been occupied by the

Nazis. Most Jews were turned away and taunted; some of them were killed. For up to ten years most of the surviving Jewish population lived in refugee camps in Europe.[2] As I stood at the holocaust exhibit, I wondered how a person who had seen the horror of Hitler's final solution could not welcome back the Jewish citizens of her village. How could she not offer a blanket or a place to stay? Why did the editors of town newspapers not welcome back the beaten and tortured members of their communities? Obviously, anti-Semitism was as potent as ever.

In all fairness, Germany and her occupied countries were devastated after the war and individuals had nothing to spare, yet this does not explain the lack of heart and the blatant anti-Semitism that continued. People did not want the Jews back; they would be forever reminded of the blemish on their history. They would have to live with Jews and see them daily—they would have to deal with anti-Semitism. The issue would have been on the table, unavoidable. The end of the war would have shown itself for what it was: the beginning point to work on anti-Semitism, German identity and the many complicated issues around power and status haunting the German nation. Instead, the shame and inability to deal with the issues encouraged a wall of silence.

Similarly, the Civil War in the United States was little more than an economic victory for the north. Although there were significant numbers of abolitionists and anti-slavery groups, they were definite minorities. Furthermore, the sad truth is that many northerners and people of power were motivated by the political and economic gains of ending the slaveocracy of the south, not by a sense that the slaves deserved freedom. After the war ended, some of the most brutal treatment of black people ensued. Blacks were no longer seen as property to be protected, and lynch mobs ruled the land, murdering thousands of black men and women. These post-war decades were also responsible for insuring the structures of institutionalized racist policy and belief.[3] The crucial issues of domination and freedom, white supremacy and racism, remained untouched for future generations to grapple with.

After war ends most of us begin to pick up the pieces of our daily existence. We deal with basic survival, food, shelter and work. Material reconstruction takes off as society rebuilds its infrastructures. The liberated slaves and victims of the concentration camps had nothing to pick up and go back to. Victimized and marginalized from the start, they remind us that reconstruction means more than material restoration. History repeats because history is virtually vacant when it comes to our forefathers and mothers engaging in the social and emotional reconstruction essential for healing.

The Call for Social Reconstruction

What responsibility does each of us bear when wars end? In my vision, I see a leader who not only can deploy weapons, but who can inspire us in our social reconstruction and personal growth as a nation. I imagine a president who gets on the radio or TV and talks directly about the issues, names the various sides in the conflict, and encourages everyone to learn about how each conflict exists in their own lives. I imagine families and communities sitting down together and learning about issues, such as racism and anti-Semitism, and exploring how these issues affect their lives and exist within each person. Beyond the content of any conflict the basic issues of oppression and freedom, supremacy and domination, revenge and abuse, are the background to war. These issues are present in our families and interpersonal relationships as well as in our communities. We should role play the polarities of conflict and learn more about each position and how it relates to us and the environment we live in.

Social reconstruction happens on many levels; in large groups, small groups, in interpersonal relationships, and within ourselves. The first examples in this essay took place in relatively large groups of 200–300 people. Small group work might happen in our families, friendships or work gatherings. Working one-to-one in relationship is a powerful mode for going more deeply into the dynamics and intricate details of conflict. Finally, learning about these basic polarities inside ourselves has the potential to create huge transformation. No matter what level we are working on, there are basic guidelines that can help us in healing the wounds of the past and addressing the pains of the present.

The "Other"

If we look inside ourselves, we discover that we are the Jews, the Blacks, the Germans and the racists. We are the communists and capitalists, the Japanese and the Koreans, the impoverished and the greedy. We are not only the ethnic identity and social role that culture and nature assign us. We are also in some way parts of everything. We have access to every role in every issue and this self-knowledge can give new meaning to social reconstruction.

One of the most essential and difficult challenges in addressing these historical issues, or any kind of conflict, is to discover the polarities we are working with. All polarities of any given issue are internal aspects of ourselves, and thus our opponents show themselves in our dreams. We cannot entirely cut them out of our lives or kill them off in wars because they are alive in the human psyche. Therefore, knowing how these polarities interact inside of ourselves, exploring their deepest drives and purpose, gives us more understanding and compassion in outer conflict. With deeper understanding we learn alternative methods of interacting with diversity besides annihilation. It takes courage, humility and heart to put our identities aside and discover the "other" in our hearts.

When we discover the "other" in ourselves, we are more prepared in interacting with this polarity in the outer world. This kind of inner work happens when we imagine a person or position we are in conflict with and discover the essence of who they are. We might ask ourselves: where is this person coming from, what is their life experience, how do they stand and hold themselves, what is the energetic or emotional quality behind their speech and actions? Then we might explore the possibility of how we might in some way embody an aspect of this "other" in ourselves. In this internal meeting, we have the opportunity to learn more about ourselves and to discover the most fruitful ways of interacting with this "other" in the outer world.

Mindell states that doing this kind of inner work preparation is crucial in working with groups of people who we disagree with, scare us, or who seem different. I remember a time when I was preparing for a meeting in which one of the parties was a fundamentalist Christian with beliefs I don't share. As I explored this public figure in my fantasy I discovered a certain confident quality that he possessed. Beneath his rhetoric was this amazing confidence and certainty. I realized that I could use some of that confidence in my own life, particularly in the world. I also recognized how I unconsciously become this fundamentalist "other" when an internal critical voice emerges dominating every aspect of my being. In those moments I am unaware of how a part of me suffers from such strong fundamentalist opinions. This experience also helped me in relating with this man. I was able to value his confidence and not just feel oppressed by it. Additionally, I was able to value my own confidence by bringing out my differences without having to put him down.

Such innerwork is essential when working with people and healing the rampant stereotypes that we all ultimately suffer from. For example, let's take the case of a man in my practice who made a racist comment about some homeless people. He discovered that his projections onto African Americans and Latinos were really aspects of himself. In fact, they were parts of himself that he needed more in his life. He had some of the perilous projections many white people have onto people of color, projections which implicitly keep institutionalized racism intact. Therefore, part of the work is to reveal the internal aspects of his racism in addition to debunking the myths of these stereotypes. This man desperately needed to connect with the parts of himself that were idle and laid back, not ambitious or interested in worldly success. Embracing this part of himself relieved him of his stereotypical mindset and opened him to new experiences in himself and in others.

Heartwork

History cannot be put behind us unless its emotional residue is fully experienced and completed. The heart does not quiet through passing laws or elapsing time. Neglecting history may lead to body symptoms as unexpressed emotion gnaws at us inwardly.[4] Any sustainable healing must reach into our hearts and effect emotional change. Without addressing the emotional and personal level of human experience, change remains superficial and peace processes are jeopardized. We need only look at the fragile peace process that has been underway in Israel for years. Various eruptions of violence have resulted in the deaths of hundreds of Jewish and Palestinian civilians, particularly when the negotiators seem to come close to resolution. On July 30, 1997, after the Islamic group Hamas sent two suicide bombers into an open market in Jerusalem, killing and injuring over a hundred people, Yassar Arafat acknowledged that the act was against the peace process. Why would a group so torn apart by war and tragedy not welcome peace? Evidently, the peace process did not include these factions in some way—their voices weren't heard, the negotiators weren't taking their point of view into consideration. Peace can only happen if peace is present. Neglected as usual, the wild card was the human heart. This uninvited guest at many a peace process seems to be the biggest obstacle, but it can also be the potential healer.

"Sweet revenge," we say. Hurt, angry, and in pain, the heart wants to lash out and give back. Does revenge heal? The way we long for it, talk about it and are swept away by it, you would think it does. But if we watch ourselves in daily courtroom battles, where seeking justice serves as revenge for our suffering, we can observe that we still agonize. The heart does not quiet. Revenge is sweet for one moment, but then what? The conflict is not resolved and the cycle continues as others feel the need to defend and hit back.

Revenge is meant to give our opponent the same agony that we had to endure. However, there is a piece that we seem to overlook in our acts of revenge. Once our opponent is as down and out and terrorized as we were, we want them to know and acknowledge how we felt. We imagine that now they will know the depths of our suffering and regret the agony they caused us. We are looking for a human reaction that will heal our wounds. Therefore, revenge is an important and rudimentary beginning at conflict work. It is the earliest impulse that draws us to engage. Revenge is an expression of the anger and pain that needs to be received. However, revenge that destroys the opponent can never make change because there is no chance for it to be taken in.

Edges of the Heart

How could anyone absorb the effects and receive the message in revenge? Especially if we have been hurt and victimized ourselves, how can we put aside our own pain and open up to the onslaught of emotion from another? This seems like a super-human prospect. However, it is surely within our reach. What stops us are edges. Edges keep us on familiar ground and inhibit smooth crossing into new territory. Edges consist of our fears, beliefs and life philosophies that concretize our identities, thereby creating boundaries to "other" or new experience.[5]

The heart is the home of human emotion, and like any home, it has an atmosphere that is familiar and comfortable and resists change. It can stiffen and freeze as we arrive at edges in our emotional life. As the vengeful one in us comes forward full of rage and pain, we come to our first edge in identifying with the shift of power. At this point, we are no longer the victim. The roles have switched and we are high on revenge, which is an emotionally powerful position. Noticing our power, we must also see the effect we can have on our opponent. In fact, in this moment we have become the opponent by giving back what we had received. However, with courage and awareness, it is at this juncture where the relationship can really evolve.

A second edge often emerges that dares realization; we become aware that we want interaction, that we need an acknowledgment. We want the opponent to know what we have experienced, and in our deepest ideals, we long for reconciliation. Our backlash is not just a meaningless eruption, but meant as a teaching, and we look for the recognition in the heart of the opponent. We long to be seen, experienced in the most profound way. The deepest concession we desire is that our opponent will know us from the inside out, be irrevocably affected, shaken by his own behavior, and seek forgiveness. To verbally express this need for interaction is an enormous task. Now that the passion of revenge has made us powerful, we are afraid to lose it. We freeze in that powerful state, never wanting to be victimized and hurt again. We also do not believe that we can really make an impact on our opponent, although we desperately want to. Our rigidity in this position will most likely have the unfortunate result of further escalation with a relationship based on cyclical revenge.

As the recipient of revenge, we encounter various edges as well. Even though we too might feel victimized and hurt, we must notice that when revenge is the mode of communication, drastic measures have been taken to get our attention. Inadvertently or intentionally, we have hurt others. If we remain stuck in our righteousness, we should be aware that we have made a tacit agreement to war. Escalation is inevitable, often resulting in deadly consequences. The Herculean edge that is rarely recognized would be to open up and listen. We might sense this as a new path to take by noticing some of the small signals that don't go along with our righteousness. For example, we might feel a little afraid or slightly guilty, even though the identity fights back, trying to ignore our fear or convince us that we have nothing to feel guilty about. We might begin to feel sad, to wonder about our opponent's loved ones. We might doubt ourselves or feel ashamed, or remember a dream in which we were open to our opponent. With self-awareness or with the assistance of a facilitator, these are all signals that would help us open up and listen. In this position, we might have an edge to acknowledge our own brutality, to discover the unconscious motives or consequences of our actions, and to feel the pain.

Feeling creates change. Devoid of emotion and human feeling, it is no wonder that mediation and diplomatic peace talks rarely deliver sustainable solutions. Going over edges brings about surprising and deep emotional change with far-reaching reverberations. In 1997, at a large seminar in India, the group focused on the divisions of India's caste system.[6] A group of Indian people asserted that caste was really no longer an issue in India; poverty was the main issue, and poverty crossed all caste barriers. There was a great discomfort in the room, an expectation of something about to happen, when suddenly two men began to wail about the pain of living as "untouchables," one of the lowest castes in Indian society. The emotional temperature in the group was hot as the men raged on. Revenge was in the air; individuals as well as the Hindu religion sustained great attacks. After the initial seconds of shock, many of the Indian people began to sob, visibly moved by the release of pent-up pain and aggression by the two men who courageously stood for their humanity against injustice. The group went further in processing the details of a conflict between one of these men and one of his colleagues of higher caste. The shared emotion brought the group together and reached deeply into the hearts of us all. Later I spoke with one the youngest participants, a woman sixteen years of age. She came from a higher caste and was unaware of the emotional reality of caste discrimination and racism in India. She was deeply moved and was going to speak out to her school friends. Such are the effects of change when the heart is moved and feeling is invited to the mediation table.

This was a rich group process in which the two men of lower caste were able to go over their edges. First they took a huge social risk in their peer group by courageously bringing a disavowed issue forward. Second, as they began to express their revenge, they realized they wanted an interaction. Later they also realized that they had become the oppressor they had suffered from and apologized to the group for disrespecting the Hindu religion. The mainstream Indian group went over an edge as well. They moved from their position that had insisted caste was a non-issue and opened up to the pain and disavowed voices around them. Both positions were very fluid, and by working publicly in front of an international group of 300 people, they were role models for us all, bringing together the international community as well as their own.

Spiritual Warriorship

To heal the wounds of history and to reduce the cycle of pain, power, and revenge, we must take a quantum leap in how we deal with conflict. We must be courageous enough to learn more than what we know and to risk emotional expression. With so few role models in our world, the concept of spiritual warriorship can be an inspiration for many of us seeking new ways to deal with old problems. Spiritual warriorship refers to an attitude toward life and toward how we approach conflict or difficulty.[7] The spiritual warrior is not interested in battle, or in winning or losing; rather, she emphasizes learning. Every conflict, surprise, dream or irritation is used to further the growth of herself and the world around her. In fact, she doesn't separate herself from the world around her, but sees herself as intricately connected to its workings. The world is really her world, regardless of whether or not she has any social status or power. She is here on a spiritual mission to follow the movements of nature and to reap as much learning as she can.

The woman or man who embraces spiritual warriorship is not confined to a social identity and is free to step into various positions in social encounters. He knows that he cannot just walk away from turmoil and retreat into a life of privilege, but that it is his obligation to engage for the progress of us all. The spiritual warrior might not like conflict, but he seems to tolerate it more easily. He holds an outside viewpoint that allows him to be in the conflict and also at times to be detached from it, knowing that he and others are more than the issue at hand. His fluidity allows him access to various parts of himself that prevent him from getting stuck in one position, and that give him compassion in dealing with others.

The spiritual warrior follows the movements of her heart and can express a diversity of feeling. She can speak for herself, but she is also able to speak for the feelings of others, even when they are contrary to her own. She knows that even if she can articulate her position clearly, she is also responsible for those who are silent and will try to feel into their position as well. She might not agree with that position, but she knows that if it goes unexpressed it will wreak havoc later and interfere with conflict work. The spiritual warrior is the perennial elder and takes the world as her children.

These ideals may be too high or unrealistic for many of us. They seem high because they are foreign and unfamiliar, but they will be necessary as we continue into the current millennium. In fact, many of us display these attributes in our lives and we have become the natural elders, healers, or inspirational leaders of our communities.

Healing and Learning

My history teacher never told us exactly what we should have learned from history. I don't think he really knew. I am attempting to show why history repeats itself and to offer some tips for our collective learning, since we all must deal with conflict and the residue of our shared history. Learning in conflict work is essential—not just learning from the past, but learning on the spot in the present conflict. Engaging in conflict with the attitude of a learner is one of the most valuable tools we can have. Healing happens when we have learned something and is the most satisfying when our opponent learns as well.

In the example from India, the vengeful man who had been so hurt by the oppression of the caste system learned a variety of things. He learned about his emotional power; that his feelings could sway a group. He also learned how that power can grab him, blinding him to others and turning him into what he detests. Many of the higher caste Indians learned about the pain of oppression and how their privilege, which allows them the comfort of unconsciousness, contributes to this oppression. These are general learnings, and I am sure that the people present had many other personal learnings and experiences.

Apologies and Forgiveness

Apologies often seem empty without learning, and are therefore difficult to simply accept. The recipient of the apology wonders, "Why did it happen, why did you do that, how can I be sure you won't do it again?" These questions must be explored in order for the heart to really open. Answering them takes some skill and an ability to go into the unknown. Chances are the "hurtful" one has no idea why she did what she did. She might even feel misunderstood. She doesn't see her whole self, doesn't see the part of her that could have been hurtful. Most of us don't mean to hurt and oppress others; we don't think of ourselves as hurtful or oppressive. We are unaware of our behavior.

The German people did not think of themselves as hurtful or oppressive. Defeated and humiliated in the First World War, many German people were unaware of their own need for power and pride. Perhaps their devastation and inferiority feelings made them open to Nazi propaganda and the rise of a nationalistic leader.

The unconscious roots of historical conflict always emerge in the present in order for us to learn more about them. They need to manifest so we can explore ourselves and make sustainable change. Therefore, the unconscious supremacy of white people must seep through in some way when we are working on issues of racism. Noting those moments and learning about the roots of that dynamic in ourselves is crucial in going further with race relations. Genuine learning produces genuine change which makes apology heartfelt and can open the heart of the receiver.

Forgiveness in many kinds of conflict seems almost impossible. Letting someone who has deeply hurt us into our heart seems beyond human reach. Opening our hearts to nations, races or groups of people who have oppressed and murdered our own might not be our task in this life. However, some people are able to do it. I don't want to advocate that anyone should, but it is truly awesome when such healing occurs. It is something like grace.

A person who has burned her own wood,[8] expressed all her rage, agony and sadness until she is empty, might begin to open up to others. Some of us are able to go so deeply into the passions of our hearts that we find ourselves coming out the other side. We find ourselves sustained by something other than our hurt and revenge. We have been through the cycles of history countless times and long for lasting reconciliation. We begin to see that our enemies are people like us, caught up in history and in need of help. We may begin to feel like an elder for the world at large, and to notice that we too hold the keys for major transformation.

I have witnessed many miraculous moments where grace must have led the way, moments that give me faith in the human race and leave me trembling. I remember the July 4th weekend of 1996 where I attended a seminar to work on Asian issues.[9] After two days of intense emotion and interaction reliving the history between Japanese, Korean and Chinese people, the last minutes floored me. The Japanese people fell to their knees in tears, apologizing to the Korean and Chinese people for past invasions and the history of oppression, murder and discrimination. They took full responsibility for the acts of their ancestors, vowed never to allow such atrocities again, and pledged to educate their children. Chinese and Korean people were deeply moved; some joined them on the floor, some embraced, and others took in this awesome scene visibly moved. Everyone in the room knew they had witnessed an extraordinary event.

Some hours later, still full with the incredible experience of the seminar, I thought of my ninth grade history class. This seminar was the kind of history class I want to attend and I want our children to attend. Learning from history means engaging in its living reality, learning together about the issues of past and present and how to work with conflict and difference. It means teaching children to value their feelings as the great resources they are. And it means picking up the legacy that has been passed on and being part of the healing of history.

End Notes

[1] See A. Elizabeth Delany, Sarah Louise Delany, and Amy Hill Hearth *Having Our Say: The Delany Sisters' First 100 Years* (New York: Delta Trade Paperbacks, 1996), in which two sisters, both over a hundred years old, recount their extraordinary lives and the racism their family encountered. Their father was an ex-slave.
[2] The Holocaust Museum serves as a memorial and historical reminder to a tragic piece of history. Some of the exhibits are there for only limited time periods.

This special exhibit focusing on liberation and the aftereffects of the war was on display in the summer of 1995.

[3] See Angela Davis, *Women, Race and Class* (New York: Vintage Books, 1983), for a review of the legacy of slavery, the anti-slavery movement, and the politics of slavery. Davis also offers a wealth of invaluable research into the important players and politics at the turning of the 19th century.

[4] See Arnold Mindell, *Sitting in the Fire.*

[5] For a description of edges see Arnold Mindell, *Working with the Dreaming Body.* For further understanding of edges in relationships and in the social sphere see Mindell's *The Dream Body in Relationships* and *Sitting in the Fire.*

[6] From March 27–April 6, 1997, The Global Process Institute held its annual worldwork seminar in Lonavala, India.

[7] Spiritual warriorship is a term that has grown out of process work, particularly in regard to relationship work and community life.

[8] Arnold Mindell made use of this expression after hearing an Israeli woman speak these words about her fury and fire and her subsequent detachment in regard to the history of the Holocaust. See *Sitting in the Fire*: 150 for another example.

[9] This seminar was held in San Francisco, California and was facilitated by Drs. Arny and Amy Mindell, pioneers in the field of conflict work. Approximately 200 people were present from all over the world. The majority of participants were from Asia or were Asian Americans.

A Marriage Made in Heaven

You were always with me. I struggled to understand the sense of breathing that seemed to follow me everywhere. I would turn around expecting to find someone behind me, but no one was there. Then I would hold my breath and try to listen at the same time, imagining that I was just hearing myself. But I still heard that unrelenting beat, its cadence predictable. Where was it coming from? It was as if the air itself were breathing. I felt the pulse, heard the faint sounds of respiration and felt the movement as a slight tug on my skin. My body seemed to sway in time as if floating in the tide of the sea. If I squinted and looked closely I thought I could see molecules floating in the air, moving, forming and disappearing. I would follow one of them, watching the trail it made, intent on finding the source, until I lost track and it disappeared into space, only to replace itself with another one.

Your breathing used to scare me but totally captivated me. I would forget about you and then, without warning in the most ordinary circumstances, you were there overwhelming my senses until your pulse was the only one present. The world seemed to stop, as all matter vibrated to the consuming rhythm. It was as if you breathed me, like a steady pull, drawing me close and then releasing me, only to gather me up again and again. At last free from your grasp, I would miss you as ordinary reality reclaimed its dominance.

Most of the time I have known you in crisis. As an adolescent when the world seemed to crumble I found you under the stars, in lonely wooded areas, and in abandoned lots piled with junk. I found refuge in a discarded cement cylinder from some building project. Large enough for me to sit in, it was a perfect place to sing out to you, the echoes vibrating my bones and filling my soul. Whether I was shaking with sobs or fuming against injustice, you received my broken heart and rocked me into soothing surrender. You emptied me, leaving your mark of serenity, and I stumbled back into time renewed.

I didn't call you by any holy name. I didn't know what to call you. I felt you. I felt you deep inside my stomach and way back behind my eyes. I didn't know if you were inside or outside me. Sometimes, I heard you in my songs or in low quiet tones. Other times I seemed to feel you in nature or see you in the gaze of a child or a solitary old man. I knew I wasn't alone even though the world felt so lonely.

Religion had names for you and fought over which name was the real name, but for me you were a nameless presence. My family didn't believe in you. We didn't pray to you and we didn't fear you. We didn't ask for your help and we didn't seek your forgiveness. My Grandfather believed in science. My Grandmother seemed to share his viewpoint, but years later intimated that perhaps there was some kind of greater force. My parents believed in family and success. They all believed in Jewish culture. My Uncle was vehemently against religion and held it responsible for most wars. He and my Aunt proudly displayed a peace sign on top of their annual Christmas tree.

Years ago when I lived in Zurich, Switzerland, I was sitting in my apartment at the kitchen table drinking coffee and reading about Hinduism. The doorbell rang. I made it down the eight flights of steps to let in the unexpected visitors. Two clean-cut young men in suits stood at my door and in perfect American English wanted to talk to me about my religious beliefs. Since I was in the midst of studying religion, I found their timing quite synchronistic and invited them to my table. They awkwardly made their way into my simple kitchen and pulled up folding chairs. They declined coffee and set out on their mission. These smooth-faced young men were out to bring me the word of God. Although I had read some about the Mormon religion, it was my first conversation with Mormon people. I marveled at the confidence and certainty these men had in talking about their religious beliefs, but I was repelled by their insistence on these beliefs for everyone and their lack of knowledge about other religious systems.

Not interested in conversion, I hoped to use the opportunity to ask these young men about divine revelation, a cornerstone of Mormon belief that had always fascinated me. The Mormon religion was inspired by the divine revelations of Joseph Smith. Central to its written philosophy is the notion that personal experience with God is accessible to each of us through our revelations. This sliver of Mormon thought had attracted me because it supported personal religious experience and a direct growing relationship with God. From this perspective religion seemed like a dynamic experience, a growing movement rather than a static institution.

Before I could get a sentence in, my guests quizzed me. "Do you believe in God?" I would have to find another way to bring in my interests. At that moment I remembered a BBC interview I had seen some years back with Carl Jung. His answer to that question had impressed me deeply and started me thinking about the human relationship to the divine.

"I don't believe. I know God," I answered, letting Jung's memory ring in my ears.

They became flustered, and then got back on their track. "But how do you know God?" they probed.

"Through my own experiences," I said.

"But how do you know your experiences are real?"

"Why should I doubt them?" I queried.

Puzzled, these young men away from home on their first holy mission, with no knowledge of my faith or experience, patiently explained to me that a prophet must confirm whether or not my experiences were true. I told them that it was not necessary to seek such validation, because I knew of their truth and value and needed no confirmation. I then asked them why someone had to confirm the existence of God for them.

"We might be led astray. Our revelation might not be of divine truth."

"Why would you let a man judge your own divinity?" I dug deeper. "Your founder believed in his divine revelation. He did not ask a man if God existed or if his revelation was real. He built a whole religion on that concept: the ability for an individual to be in direct contact with God, to have divine revelation."

They explained to me that the later prophets had to confirm their revelations with the prophets who came before. They challenged me, "You can't possibly believe in your own revelations, they could come from the devil!" I told them that I wouldn't wish to condemn anyone's inner experience, that it is precious and a divine gift. "It is only man who judges between good and evil, inflating himself as if he were a God," I asserted.

Exasperated and hopeless, they sighed, left some literature on the table, and said they had other appointments.

Revelation or no revelation, the Mormon religion seemed to me like many other organized religious structures that inhibited and evaluated spontaneous spiritual experience. Dreams, visions and natural eruptions of the heart could not just be experienced, but had to be confirmed by a holy man. Someone else had to have had the experience first. Doubt first, ask if it is real, and determine whether the experience fits into the established canon. Everyday reality is not questioned and evaluated for its merits or validity, but spontaneous expression of the human spirit is. From this perspective, the religious institution is static and predetermined rather than a reflection of the growing and dynamic presence of spirit.

When did I start to doubt my inner experiences and worship the world of known reality? When did I begin to look outside myself for validation and to depend on it as the sole source for my well-being? How is it that I could be so overwhelmed by your grace only to fall back into the hypnotic world of material experience? I didn't learn the patience and reverence to sit with that with which I did not know. I didn't learn to court mystery, to unfold hidden meanings and probe ancient wisdom. I learned to fix and adjust life's unpredictable expressions, thinking I could shape them into something familiar. I learned that nature was to be tamed and conquered; that the collective dominance of consensus reality was to be maintained at all costs. I learned to fear the unknown in its natural and psychic forms. And I learned that my soul had been robbed.

It is not that I had stopped believing in you; without you, life was hollow and functional, lacking soul and substance. But what does it take to breathe you from the inside? To know that my breath is yours, that my vision is your sight and that the impulse behind my movement originates with you? I have yearned for that attention, a divine lens that endows perception with a sacred glow, a focus that is at home and alert in the wilderness of life.

I mistook you for a lover. Consumed by my need for love, I betrayed you. I fell comfortably into human arms and rested my hopes, dreams and sense of well being in her. I searched for you in her eyes and longed to feel you in our sex. You waited like a mistress in the wings, certain I would return, dreaming that you would one day take your rightful place. I knew you were there. I knew who held my bones and breathed my cells. Your patience was eternal.

When her arms no longer held me and our bond was broken, I fell to the bottom. Hurt, angry and devastated to lose the woman of my dreaming, I wailed in agony. I struck out against fate, raging at the stars for taking love. I sobbed myself into oblivion and was convinced love would never find me again. But who was I kicking? Who absorbed the intensity of my fury? Who listened to my cries and collected my tears at night? I was interacting with someone, something, some being who could hear, touch and meet me.

In the midst of my emotional fervor, I heard your voice rumble up from the bowels of my being. "I am number one!" Startled and confused, I became quiet, trying to comprehend the madness coming through me. "I am number one," you repeated. "Marry me." This was crazy. "I don't want to marry you. I want to be a normal woman. I want true love, home and security, and arms of flesh around me. I don't want to be married to a spirit!" I shouted back at you. "I come first," you countered with resolute calm, observing my protest.

There was no way out. I screamed and flailed and tried to negotiate, all to no avail. You were claiming what was yours; you had come for your beloved. It was time. You had heard my cries and felt my anguish. Your certainty began to work on me. You were the spirit behind human love gone awry, and you threw me a life-line. The struggle subsided and I began to relax into a fate I always knew would one day possess me. A clear and independent center, calm and lucid, took hold. My heart rested.

Our marriage began with a honeymoon I could never have predicted. You held my naked heart as it miraculously pieced itself together again. Suspended by starlight, my heavy load lifted. I walked the world free and easy, almost reckless. I felt cut loose and fearless; nothing seemed to phase me. I was free. Ordinary reality could no longer contain me.

Our union was sanctified and I felt blessed. Your eyes merged with mine and I felt the eternal warmth of your undying love. For months I was joyously consumed in your grasp, until its intensity faded and my small-minded ways began to flirt with me again. I became greedy, coveting past ecstasies, inadequate to meet your daily challenges to cultivate new awareness. I could hardly sustain your lucid and loving focus. Estrangement fell upon our union and I longed for you. You retreated to the wings until I would open my doors for you again.

You are a challenging partner and want nothing less than my total devotion to my own growth and awareness. I am not faithful, not because I don't want to be. The familiar routine of unconscious doing possesses me and I abandon the rapture of your sentient stillness. Your focus should be as effortless as my unconsciousness. Instead it too can become corrupted by a loveless discipline that lacks spirit and becomes a chore.

I need crisis, and I detest it, dread the pain and upheaval. But I need those times when my entire identity is wiped out, when the world of doing becomes irrelevant and you come rushing from the wings to occupy the place that has been cleared out for you. Secure in our chambers I effortlessly follow your lead and our love thrives. I am renewed by these exceptional and extreme times, when the world stops and I am relieved of its demands and routines, when my compulsive self-loathing is obliterated and each second pulses with the vitality of your awareness.

Crisis has never been a test to my faith. I never thought of divorcing you, holding you responsible for the painful and tragic, a pious Job absorbing the onslaughts of life's travails to prove devotion. I never expected a God to be different from the multitudinous expressions of nature. Your will is not synonymous with mine. Therefore, how could I condemn you for not fulfilling my needs, or for failing to carve out a carefree existence? I think people test you. Will you deliver? Will you meet the needs and desires of the victimized and greedy, hopeless and skeptical? I don't think you do tests. Tests are for showmen who believe in their own centrality as the voice of God. They prove human supremacy but do not challenge us to go beyond what we already know, or to penetrate the deeper mysteries and unpredictable nature of life.

Like the holy and enlightened ones have always said, you work in mysterious ways. Therefore, your nature defies all tests. You hold to no linear or rational route and are detached from human morals. Your nature is mercurial and yet we seem to worship only the predictable and tangible. We worship the material, the creation itself, the idol, and your eternal essence slips through our grasp. Being close to you means following the ever-changing path of experience as it emerges. It means embracing our constantly evolving natures. You are an experience, not a form, a mystery that leads us to the borders of what we know. You are our capacity for extraordinary transformation. To embrace your nature is to embrace my own. What an awesome challenge you present; to be a conscious part of our constantly changing evolution, to co-create and learn. It is the greatest gift of living.

When we are down and suffering and pray to you, we seem to ask you to alter the events of our lives, to change the course of our luck. The events of living come and go, but your powers lie in how we get along with these circumstances. You emerge in our ability to transform everyday life, to penetrate beyond its painful or mundane trappings. In this sense, crisis is not a test, but an awesome opportunity. We are holy vessels able to transform the chaotic and horrific, to thrive and develop regardless of circumstance. We discover your grace and the sacred power of our own spirits when we face incredible odds and challenges and grow beyond the immediate. We suffer the hardships but reap unfathomable rewards that alter our inner states and offer the potential for great transformation.

I do not want to wait for the extreme junctures in life when my will is wiped out and you can finally get through. Crisis is easy; the intensity and drama eventually drop me into your arms. But I search for you daily. I long to find you as a young child does, in each moment, possessed by wonder and curiosity as I approach each experience anew. You are a way of life, of breathing, seeing and feeling. You are the creative spirit inspiring me on the path of constant discovery.

I now know why I had no name for you. A name defines you, keeps your mercurial nature under the yoke of human will. I understand the ancient Hebrews who would not utter your name, the Taoists who claim your powers lie in the Tao that cannot be spoken, and the Hindus who have so many names for the great diversity of your unfathomable nature. The capacity for your expression is limitless and can never be pinned down. Young children know this. They effortlessly court you until they grow older and become consumed by consensus reality. Depression sinks in; we devalue our deepest experiences, or we hardly notice them and life loses meaning. When we support our growing children to value the totality of their experiences and to believe in their spontaneous perceptions, we are parenting the original core of the human spirit and making way for the infinite and awesome.

Our union does not take place in a holy building, but in the untamed chambers of my heart. Here you personally reveal yourself to me, and my identity melts as I yield to the uncanny workings of your mystery. I am learning to take my vows seriously; our marriage is what really sustains me. All of my deepest longings lead me to you. You are the seed from which my ambitions germinate. You are the only constant, a true and eternal love.

References and Additional Reading

Allison, Dorothy, *Skin: Talking about Sex, Class and Literature.* Ithaca: Firebrand, 1994.

Bauerlein, Monika, "The Unkindest Cut," *The Utne Reader,* No. 77, October 1996 issue.

Berman, Paul, ed., *Blacks and Jews.* New York: Dell Publishing, 1995.

Billingsley, Andrew, *Climbing Jacob's Ladder: The Enduring Legacy of African-American Families.* New York: Simon and Schuster, 1992.

Blofield, John, *Taoism: The Road to Immortality.* Boston: Shambhala, 1985.

Brown, Rita Mae, *Sudden Death.* New York: Bantam Books, 1984.

Castaneda, Carlos, *The Teachings of Don Juan.* Berkeley: University of California Press, 1968.

Castaneda, Carlos, *A Separate Reality.* New York: Simon and Schuster, 1971.

Castaneda, Carlos, *Journey to Ixtlan.* New York: Simon and Schuster, 1972.

Castaneda, Carlos, *Tales of Power.* New York: Simon and Schuster, 1974.

Chesler, Phyllis, *Women and Madness.* Garden City, New York: Doubleday, 1972.

Davis, Angela, *Women, Race and Class.* New York: Vintage Books, 1983.

Delaney, A. Elizabeth and Sarah Louise, and Amy Hill Hearth, (Contributor), *Having Our Say: The Delaney Sisters' First 100 Years.* New York: Delta Trade Paperbacks, 1996.

Eck, Diana, *Encountering God: A Spiritual Journey from Bozeman to Banaras*. Boston: Beacon Press, 1993.

Ehrenreich, Barbara and English, Deirdre, *For Her Own Good: 150 Years of the Expert's Advice to Women*. Garden City, NY: Anchor Press/Doubleday, 1978.

Evans-Wentz, W.Y., ed., *The Tibetan Book of the Dead*. London: Oxford University Press, 1960.

Feinberg, Leslie, *Stone Butch Blues*. Ithaca, NY: Firebrand, 1993.

Flexner Eleanor, *Century of Struggle: The Women's Rights Movement in the U.S.* New York: Atheneum, 1973.

Fulop-Miller, Rene, *Saints that Moved the World*. Salem, NH: Ayer Company, Reprint Edition, 1991.

Goodbread, Joseph, *The Dreambody Toolkit*. London: Routledge and Kegan Paul, 1987.

Goodbread, Joseph, *Radical Intercourse: How Dreams Unite Us in Love, Conflict and Other Inevitable Relationships*. Portland, OR: Lao Tse Press, 1997.

Guirand, Felix, ed., *The New Larousse Encyclopedia of Mythology*. New York: Hamlyn Limited, 1959.

Hadden, Jeffrey and Shupe, Anson, eds., *Prophetic Religions and Politics*. New York: Paragon House, 1984.

Hanh, Thich Naht, *Being Peace*. Berkeley, CA: Parallax Press, 1988.

Halprin, Sara, *Look at My Ugly Face*. New York: Viking, 1995.

Harvey, Andrew, *Hidden Journey*. New York: Henry Holt, 1991.

Hoch-Smith, J. and Spring, A. eds., *Women in Ritual and Symbolic Roles*. New York: Plenum Press, 1978.

hooks, bell, *Teaching to Transgress: Education as the Practice of Freedom*. New York and London: Routledge, 1994.

hooks, bell, *Killing Rage*. New York: Henry Holt, 1995.

hooks, bell, *Bone Black: Memories of Girlhood*. New York: Henry Holt, 1996.

James, William, *The Varieties of Religious Experience*. Cambridge: Harvard University Press, 1961.

The Journal of Process Oriented Psychology, Featuring Politics and Process Work. Portland, OR: Lao Tse Press, 1995: Vol. 7, No. 1.

The Journal of Process Oriented Psychology, Featuring Worldwork. Portland, OR: Lao Tse Press, 1993 Vol. 5, No. 1.

The Journal of Process Oriented Psychology, Featuring Extreme States of Consciousness Portland, OR: Lao Tse Press, 1993: Vol. 6, No. 1.

Jung, C.G., *Answer to Job.* London: Routledge and Kegan Paul, 1954.

Jung, C.G., *The Collected Works of C.G. Jung, Psychology and Religion,* Vol. 11, Bollingen Series XX. Princeton: Princeton University Press, 1958.

Jung, C.G., *The Collected Works of C.G. Jung, The Archetypes and the Collective Unconscious,* Vol. 9, Part I, Bollingen Series XX. Princeton: Princeton University Press, 1959.

Kivel, Paul, *Uprooting Racism: How White People Can Work for Racial Justice.* Gabriola Island, BC: New Society Publishers, 1995.

Kochman, Thomas, *Black and White Styles in Conflict.* Chicago: Chicago University Press, 1981.

Lazare Bernard, *Anti-Semitism: Its History and Causes.* Lincoln: University of Nebraska, 1995.

Lerner, Michael and West, Cornell, *Jews and Blacks.* New York: Grosset/Putnam, 1995.

Lorde, Audre, *Sister Outsider.* Freedom, CA: The Crossing Press Feminist Series, 1984.

McCall, Nathan, *Makes Me Wanna Holler.* New York: Vintage Books, 1994.

Menken, Dawn, "*Emerging World Views: Cultural Transformation in Process Oriented Psychology.*" Diss., Union Institute, Cincinnati, Ohio, 1989.

Merton, Thomas, *The Way of Chuang Tzu.* New York: New Directions Books, 1969.

Miller, Niela, *Counseling in Genderland.* Boston: Different Path Press, 1996.

Mindell, Amy, *Metaskills: The Spiritual Art of Therapy.* Tempe, AZ: New Falcon Publications, 1995.

__________, *Coma: A Healing Journey: A Guide for Family, Friends, and Helpers.* Portland, OR: Lao Tse Press, 1999.

Mindell, Arnold, *Dreambody: The Body's Role in Revealing the Self.* Boston: Sigo Press, 1982.

___________, *Working with the Dreaming Body*. Boston and London: Routledge and Kegan Paul, 1985.

___________, *River's Way: The Process Science of the Dreambody*. Boston and London: Routledge and Kegan Paul, 1985.

___________, *The Dreambody in Relationships*. London: Routledge and Kegan Paul, 1987.

___________, *City Shadows: Psychological Interventions in Psychiatry*. London: Routledge and Kegan Paul, 1988.

___________, *Coma: Key to Awakening*. Boston: Shambhala, 1989.

___________, *The Year I: Global Process Work*. London: Arkana, 1989.

___________, *Leader as Martial Artist: Techniques and Strategies for Resolving Conflict and Creating Community*. San Francisco: Harper Collins, 1992.

___________, *The Shaman's Body*. San Francisco: Harper, 1993.

___________, *Sitting in the Fire: Large Group Transformation Using Conflict and Diversity*. Portland, OR: Lao Tse Press, 1995.

Morgan, Sally, *My Place*. Western Australia: Fremantle Arts Center Press, 1987.

Oakley, Ann, *Woman's Work: The Housewife Past and Present*. New York: Vintage Books, 1976.

Otto, Rudolf, *The Idea of the Holy*. New York: Oxford University Press, 1958.

Owen, Lara, *Her Blood is Gold: Celebrating the Power of Female Menstruation*. San Francisco: Harper, 1993.

Neihardt, John, *Black Elk Speaks*. New York: Pocket Books, 1972.

Paglia, Camille, *Sex, Art and American Culture*. New York: Vintage Books, 1992.

Peck, Scott, *The Different Drum: Community Making and Peace*. New York: Simon and Schuster, 1987.

Porter, Bill, *Road to Heaven: Encounters with Chinese Hermits*. San Francisco, Mercury House, 1993.

Rinpoche, Sogyal, *The Tibetan Book of Living and Dying*. San Francisco: Harper, 1992.

Ryan, Mary, P., *Womanhood in America*. New York: New Viewpoints, 1975.

Sapphire, *Push*. New York: Alfred A. Knopf, 1996.

Signorile, Michelangelo, *Queer in America: Sex, the Media and the Closets of Power.* New York: Random House, 1993.

Sinclair, April, *Ain't Gonna Be the Same Fool Twice.* New York: Avon Books, 1996.

Smith, H., *The Religions of Man.* New York: Harper and Row, 1958.

Souljah, Sister, *No Disrespect.* New York: Vintage Books, 1994.

Stanton, Elizabeth Cady, Anthony, Susan B., and Gage Matilda Joslyn, *History of Woman Suffrage,* Vol. 1. New York: Fowler and Wells, 1881.

Ussher, Jane, *Women's Madness: Misogeny or Mental Illness?* Amherst, University of Massachusetts Press, 1992.

Muktananda, Swami, *The Play of Consciousness.* Camp Meeker, CA: SYDA Foundation, 1974.

Riley, Glenda, *Divorce: An American Tradition.* New York: Oxford University Press, 1991.

Sontag, F. and Bryant, M.D., *God: The Contemporary Discussion.* New York: The Rose of Sharon Press, 1982.

Takaki, Ronald, *A Different Mirror: A History of Multicultural America.* Boston: Little Brown & Co., 1993.

Tzu, Lao, *Tao Te Ching,* trans. D.C. Lau. New York: Penguin, 1963.

Walker, Alice and Parmar, Pratibha, *Warrior Marks: Female Genital Mutilation and the Sexual Blinding of Women.* New York: Harcourt Brace and Company, 1993.

Welch, Holmes, *Taoism: The Parting of the Way.* Boston: Beacon Press, 1957.

West, Cornell, *Race Matters.* New York: Vintage Books, 1994.

Wilhelm, Richard, trans., *I Ching or Book of Changes.* London: Routledge and Kegan Paul, 1951.

Zaehner, R.C., ed., *The Concise Encyclopedia of Living Faiths.* Boston: Beacon Press, 1967.

Zinn, Howard, *A People's History of the United States.* New York: Harper and Row, 1980.